Jobbing

Un-
Jobbing

The Adult Liberation Handbook

Michael Fogler

FREE CHOICE PRESS
Lexington, Kentucky

Cataloging-in-Publication Data
Fogler, Michael.
    Un-jobbing : the adult liberation handbook / Michael Fogler
      p. cm.
    Includes organizational and bibliographical references.
    ISBN 0-9654834-0-1
    1. Saving and thrift. 2. Finance, Personal. 3. Simplicity. 4. Conduct of
life. I. Title.
640.4   96-86570

DEDICATION

to all those on Earth who believe in love, unity, honesty, purpose, and environmental responsibility more than paychecks.

ACKNOWLEDGEMENTS

I acknowledge and express my deepest gratitude to the people who have had a profound effect on my life and thus a profound effect on the writing of this book—my wife, Suzanne McIntosh, my son, Benjamin, and my parents, JoAnn and Irving Fogler. I particularly wish to thank and acknowledge David Thomson, Bob Crovo, Suzanne McIntosh, and Kathy Brown for the many hours they each devoted to copy editing, proof reading, and commenting for this book at various stages of development.

I extend my thanks to my local librarian, Diana Seidel, for helping me with the Cataloging-in-Publication Data, to JoAnn and Jared Fitzpatrick for their work with the cover design, and to my photographer friend, Kesler Stivers, for donating his time to shoot the author photo.

In addition, many friends have given me encouragement and support for getting this book out. I especially acknowledge the support and friendship of Jean Givens, David Thomson, Neil Chethik, Ed Pearson, Ann Marx, and Mac Hudson as well as dozens of people who have taken my workshops on Voluntary Simplicity.

Contents

Foreword 1

Chapter 1 — Why This Book? 3

Chapter 2 — A Babyboomer's Story 15

Chapter 3 — About "Making a Living" 25

Chapter 4 — A Different View of Economics 37

Chapter 5 — How Much Is Your Job *Costing* You 47

Chapter 6 — What Would Be Better: Higher Income or

Lower Expenses? 56

Chapter 7 — (Unlike Death) Taxes Are Not Certain 74

Chapter 8 — The Gamble of Insurance 82

Chapter 9 — Your Conscious Plan for Liberation 90

Afterword 105

Appendix 107

ABOUT THE AUTHOR

Born in 1953, Michael Fogler's former life and identity was that of a faculty member at several college music departments in the Central Kentucky area. He has also been an academic advisor at the University of Kentucky's College of Arts and Sciences.

Eschewing career labeling and orientation, Fogler now calls himself a "semi-retired stay-at-home-Dad, freelance musician, writer, and peace activist." A classically-trained guitarist, he spends much of his time in peace and justice endeavors and homeschooling with his son. He is a part-time Director for The Central Kentucky Council for Peace and Justice, a coalition of some 20 organizations in the Lexington area. Much of his work for that organization involves being Editor/Producer of its monthly newsletter, *Peaceways.* He leads seminars and workshops on peacemaking, nonviolence, cultural diversity, and voluntary simplicity in his local area.

His many interests include music, nonviolence, environmentally-sustainable living, vegetarianism, human and animal rights, race relations, spirituality, the men's movement, "unschooling" for children, and the cooperative movement. *Un-Jobbing* is his first book.

Fogler enjoys his home-based life with his wife Suzanne McIntosh and son Benjamin in Lexington, Kentucky.

FOREWORD

A funny thing happened on the way to getting this book published. The first publishing house editor who became seriously interested in the manuscript liked it so much that she quit her job! "It worked," she reported in a letter to me in response to reading the manuscript. Then she signed her letter "thanks for the inspiration, Managing Editor (until Thursday)." After she left, no one else in that publishing house had the same degree of interest in this book that she had.

Later, another publisher was ready to sign a contract with me. But a life-threatening illness forced him to decide to retire rather than publish one last book—mine. A third very interested publisher wanted revisions to the manuscript, some of which I liked and some of which I didn't like. In the meantime, months and months were passing, and the "voluntary simplicity" movement was beginning to be noticed by mainstream society. This topic was becoming of great interest to many, many people; and I was eager to add this contribution to the growing list of offerings on this subject.

Finally, I decided to publish the book myself. I had always

considered, but hesitated to choose, this time-consuming, yet valid option. Mainly, I didn't want to complicate my life greatly by publishing and selling a book about simplifying life! Walking the fine line of having a life in balance with meaningful work, play, and community is not easy in modern western society.

Indeed, that's the very challenge addressed by this book. We all want real meaning in our lives; and we don't want to stress ourselves to death to find it. My guess is that, by picking up this book, you have interest in this challenge. My hope is that *Un-Jobbing* will provide you with information, ideas, and inspiration to move your life in the direction of more balance and greater personal meaningfulness than you have now.

I will say repeatedly throughout this book that, like snowflakes, no two people or no two families are exactly alike. Your task in reading this book is to take the ideas and personal examples offered and use or modify them to suit your own specific situation. Some personal and philosophical ideas you may like, and some you may not like. There is no right or wrong—only individual choices. In addition, some ideas will make you think of other ideas that are not here. The Afterword and the Appendix will offer tips and resources, in the form of organizations and books, for further exploration.

Thus, *Un-Jobbing* is intended to be a brief, easily accessible "jump-start" for your own personal journey in the direction of meaningful and joyful simplicity. Use what you like, discard what you don't, and creatively move toward other sources and in the direction and style that speaks to you.

May this book play a helpful part in your journey toward an ever more balanced and fulfilled life of joy, peace, and love.

CHAPTER 1

WHY THIS BOOK?

Your Life = Your Job.

Do you ever get the feeling that the above is what contemporary life boils down to? The statement is somewhat of an exaggeration, but if you're a member of a modern, western industrial society, there's also a great deal of truth to it.

While children, we are sent to school whose primary purpose is to prepare us for the "adult world"—read: having a job, and, at first, being able to get a job. Then, we become adults; and we spend the bulk of our waking hours in our jobs. What we "do for a living" is our major handle or self-identity in life. One is a plumber, or an attorney, or a car dealer. And then, we retire from our jobs. Now one becomes a retired plumber, or a retired attorney, or a retired car dealer. And, that's about it. That's a thumbnail sketch of life as we know it here in late twentieth century western civilization.

In a large sense, life = job.

Are we serious? Do we really want to equate that precious commodity known as one's life with an all-consuming vocational activity which may be only mildly interesting and whose most important feature is that it is attached to a paycheck? How have we gotten to the point where "making a living" so saturates our lives that we have somehow forgotten about simply living?

These are the questions with which we urgently need to deal at the close of the twentieth century. "Life" in our culture has become almost equivalent to "job." The unfortunate thing is that "job" is too often lacking in personal fulfillment and too often over-taxing on the environment. Now that we've tried the "jobbing" world as we know it for the better part of a couple of centuries, and we see the results it has produced, I propose we try "un-jobbing."

UN-JOBBING: A NEW PROPOSAL

What do I mean by *un-jobbing*? Am I recommending that we all quit our jobs? And, if so, how do we pay for food and housing and our cars and...? ! Certainly, the latter question is constantly on the minds of people in our modern western culture, even when there is no danger of losing one's job. It's typical for most westerners to do a great deal of worrying about having the money to pay for food, housing, transportation, and other expenses. This is a book with different ideas about how one "pays the bills." Our conventional thinking on this has produced a great deal of money changing hands, a great deal of debt for many people (and governments), a great deal of environmental devastation, and—perhaps most importantly— a great deal of dissatisfaction among people about their lives. I would dare go so far as to say that there are a great many wasted lives in modern western society. We've tried the "jobbing" way of living our lives. It's now time to look in another direction. Call it "un-jobbing."

What's involved with "un-jobbing"?

First things first. I'm not necessarily advocating that you quit your job, committing a kind of economic suicide. Although by the time you finish this book you may well see that choice as quite feasible and sane. At the very least, I think we can make "occupations" much less of a pre-occupation in our lives, and be much happier at the same time.

I also see no problem with the "work ethic"—*if* we define "work" as the noted author-priest Matthew Fox did: *the joyful returning of one's gift(s) to the community.* That is the sort of "work ethic" which could change the world for the better. If only that were what we really mean when we talk about the "work ethic." But it isn't. When we use the term "work ethic," what we are really talking about is a competitive *"job* ethic;" and that is the real problem.

Plainly and simply, we take our jobs too seriously; and they are unduly dominating and consuming our lives, while, worse still, not giving us a sense of purpose and fulfillment at the same time. As a therapist I heard on National Public Radio said, "We, as a society, are suffering from terminal profession-alism." Our obsession with our jobs is contributing in a significant way to just about every major personal, local, national, and global problem you could name—either directly or indirectly—from our stressed-out family lives to our threat-ened environment.

Unfortunately, our collective society keeps thinking that we can "business" our way out of these societal and environmental problems. We cry out for help using the phrase "create jobs." It sounds as if jobs come out of thin air by magic, and then, if a person has one, he or she will automatically have a satisfactory life. We say, "*somebody* needs to help us—either the government or *somebody*—and 'create' jobs!"

Let's think again.

THE MYTH OF JOB "CREATION"

Jobs are agreements to perform work for which people are paid money. The money has to come from somewhere. It doesn't appear by magic; it is not "created" out of thin air. The money comes from all of us—either in the form of taxes we pay to governments or in the form of our own personal spending—as we buy the products or services generated by the jobs. Therefore, jobs aren't "created," they're *bought.* And, they're bought by all of us. The more we buy others' jobs with our own job-earned money, the more pressure there is on everyone's job to make more job-earned money. When people wisely stop buying so much, suddenly fewer jobs are "created" and we're in a "recession." (See more discussion on this in Chapter IV.) It's truly a vicious circle; and we're stuck in this circle going round and round and round.

Job "creation" as a solution to improve society is pure myth. This myth cannot possibly be the answer to inequality or injustice in the world—it's too competitive to be just. It surely isn't the answer to healing the environment, no matter how "green" the jobs are. Indeed, *all* economic activity has some environmental impact. And the myth of job "creation" surely isn't the answer to achieve a life of happiness and fulfillment. That seems clear. "Job" may equal "life," but it's definitely not tantamount to happiness or fulfillment.

What we have going with our jobbing orientation is a chronic national busy-ness (alias "business"), which has proven itself to be unhealthful for humans and our planetary home. We must look in another direction. We must put less emphasis on jobs and more on cooperation, simplicity, and serving one another. This may very well involve meaningful *work*, but that's not the same as *jobs*.

WHAT *DO* WE REALLY WANT IN LIFE?

It's interesting what is revealed when people are asked what they *really* want out of life. For example, Co-op America Executive Director, Alisa Gravitz, makes presentations to groups and often asks people just that. She asks in particular: how can we create a just and sustainable society? In other words, what is the kind of society which provides everyone with a happy and secure life, while, at the same time, ensures the healthy survival of our species and the planet?

Gravitz asks people to draw their own answers. The results are amazing. It seems that no matter where she is, or who is in the group—young people in an inner city, activists at a retreat center, business people in a fancy hotel—the pictures all look very much alike.

People draw a nice house representing comfort, quality of life, and economic security. They draw their family and friends relaxing or playing outside their homes, sometimes sitting together at a picnic, often in a green yard or garden. There is always lots of green, and often clean, blue water. In short, Gravitz reports, they picture themselves in a world of "family, friends, home, community, blue sky, clean air, clean water, good food."

Sounds wonderful; but if she were to ask people to draw a picture of their lives *as they are now*, it's doubtful that many of those pictures would be similar to their original pictures. So, the question is: if "family, friends, home, community, blue sky, clean air, clean water, and good food" are so treasured and valued by us, then why aren't we living our lives geared toward those ideals? Must we spend our entire lives creating societal values which are not what we truly want?

Indeed, what I'm really doing with this little book is *questioning*. I'm questioning what the late twentieth century western (particularly the United States) way of life has become. This way of life has become dominated by *jobs*, not meaningful, fulfilling *work*. Many of us see our jobs, first and foremost, as ways of making money, how we "pay the bills;" we commonly find them only superficially interesting (if that), and there is little of Fox's "joyful returning of our gifts to the community." In addition, our adult lives are so *dominated* by our jobs that our jobs have virtually *become* our lives. Even in childhood before we enter a career, our lives are mostly focused on preparing us for this kind of adulthood.

I contend there is something dreadfully wrong with this picture. But first, let me say that if you have a full-time job which you love *dearly*, which you would want to be doing *for its own sake*, even if the pay were far less than it is, and you feel 100% good about what the product or service is, then this may not be the book for you. You are a fortunate and relatively rare person in our society.

However, if you wonder why you get up early in the morning at least five days a week, and spend all day in the same perhaps mildly interesting routine, come home tired and somewhat bored, and then, after an all-too-short evening, get up early the next day to start the whole process all over again; and if you wonder why you're planning to do this week after week, month after month, year after year until your "senior years" of retirement—if you question all that, even just the least little bit in the most quiet and private of ways, then this book *is* for you. I hope you will now consider this idea of ***un-jobbing***—*letting go of the pre-occupation with, and self-inflicted domination and life-consumption by, an "occupation," while consciously and joyfully reclaiming life.*

QUESTIONS

The philosophy of *un-jobbing* asks us to question many things:

- What is the *purpose* of our lives? Why are we here?
- If you had no need for money, what would you be doing?
- Does the activity at which you spend the bulk of your waking hours *further* what you feel is your purpose for being here on Earth? And, if not, is there not something amiss here?
- Do you enjoy that activity (that is, *do you feel joyful doing it*)?
- Does this activity "feed" you?
- Is this activity sustainable for the planet?

9

• How much are we really taking responsibility for ourselves (as opposed to relying on massive bureaucratic institutions to bail us out of our problems)?

Un-jobbing is about questioning the high degree of competitiveness in our society and the high degree of separateness which that competitive attitude brings into society. Real community gets lost when we're steeped in "every man (or woman) for himself (or herself)." *Un-jobbing* is also about questioning the vast amount of environmental devastation done in the name of jobs and "economic growth," a fallacious concept which lies at the heart of much of our present-day malaise and bodes ill for the future.

Certainly, one of the main points of this philosophy is that all things are truly *connected*—that whatever you do with one aspect of your life, particularly such a large part of your life as your job, that aspect has an enormous effect upon the rest of your life. That effect extends to your family and associates, into your community, and even—very definitely—around the entire planet.

In fact, our world has drastically and dramatically changed in the last couple of centuries, more so, perhaps, than in any other two hundred year period in planetary history. (I will discuss this in more detail in Chapter III.) This has not happened by accident. It has happened because of incredibly fast-changing decisions about our lifestyles. We've all been a participant in these changing decisions. Despite the fact that they have happened *very* quickly, historically-speaking, they are so ingrained in us that few stop to question whether the current societally-assumed way of spending one's life is the best for individuals, families, communities, nations, or planets.

I didn't question it for many years. But, once I did, and I stepped off the 9 to 5 to 65 merry-go-round, I began to see clearly plenty of absurdities behind this conventional wisdom.

AN UN-JOBBED, HOME-BASED LIFE

Now, I have a completely home-based life, working independently and part-time for a "good cause" non-profit organization and doing other free-lance activities. When asked, "What do you *do*?" I reply (somewhat with tongue in cheek) that I'm a "semi-retired" free-lance musician and peace activist. (I was born in 1953.) When someone asks me, after hearing about my life, "But how do you make a living?", I usually answer: "I don't." And, indeed, in the conventional sense of this society, I don't "make a living."

I have time to spend with my family—a young child and a wife, who, though not a "homemaker," also has a home-based life. Our income is below the taxable minimum, and yet we "make ends meet" and can easily "pay the bills." We live in a wonderful middle class home (and no, I didn't inherit a lot of money). I'm unabashedly not working myself to death, and I'm not interested in "getting ahead," engaging in economic competition with others, or being "better off" (to use the politicians' economic slogan) than I was four years ago or than my parents are. I'm especially not interested in these things just because society seems to be telling me that I should be. I am very satisfied with this lifestyle.

What I *am* doing is making a meaningful contribution to

the world (at the very least it's meaningful to me) by returning my gifts back to the collective community. I'm living a lifestyle that is, relative to the American norm, light on the Earth. I have enough time to "smell the roses" and enjoy my family and friends—at least to the extent that my friends have the time to be with me. I enjoy being able to really *live* (that is, spend significant time) in my house. I have a very active, full life, but it is much more tailored to my joys, my gifts, and my interests, while also being more connected with my community, than most people's lives are.

I believe that all of this is possible for virtually everyone, and my intention with this book is to provide you, the reader, a philosophical basis, practical suggestions, and personal insights to help you move in a similar direction. There are a growing number of people who are doing one variation or another of the kinds of things which I espouse in this book. More and more people are realizing that much of what they are being fed by the "cultural line" is *literally robbing them of their lives.* By looking in another direction, we can truly reclaim our lives.

On the practical side, I plan to discuss many aspects of conventional life—from taxes to insurance to monthly financial planning to the whole fallacious philosophy of economic "growth." And, along with that, I will offer ideas for alternatives which will offer you ways to reclaim a life of family, friends, home, community, and a clean environment.

Yes, I'm advocating a radical way of living for this part of the world. It involves great nonconformity in a culture which breeds "worker bees" with a factory mentality. Of course, those who make changes like the ones described in this book may experience difficult obstacles as they begin running counter to some of the strong currents in our culture. I know that I did, and still do. The power and influence of mass culture is great indeed.

But, the institution of "making a living" has gotten way out of hand. It has been the proverbial pot of water slowly rising in temperature until the unaware frog (us) inside it boils to death at a certain point. Our cultural obsession with jobs and consumption/production is literally consuming our lives, our relationships, our communities, and our larger societies. Ultimately, it could consume our existence on this planet as a species.

We, as a society, need to go in another direction. We can keep going in the direction we have been heading; but that will only take us precisely where we are going. And where we are going is a place where there likely will be some violent transition times because we are getting closer and closer to the limits of Nature (with a capital "N") and its inherent sanity. Nature shows us time and time again that it *always* ultimately prevails. *How* it prevails is largely up to us. If we change our lives by our own free choice to something more balanced, more relaxed, more joy- and love-oriented, and more environmentally responsible, then this transition will be much more peaceful. And, we will be in sync with nature—both Nature with a capital "N" and our own nature. With un-jobbing we can reclaim our true lives *and* make our ends meet. Un-jobbing means fulfillment, freedom, flexibility, liberation, and simplicity—all with having basic needs met. It's well worth it; and it's urgently important for our time.

For now, though, try to table all of the "but what about's"

that might be floating around in your mind. Questions about a radical premise such as this are fitting. And, I fully intend to deal with at least the large, major questions that people will have about this. If I don't deal with a primary question you have, I believe that, with the resources in the Appendix, you will find the help that you need.

Before we deal with those questions, though, let me tell you my story—how I came to lead the kind of life I do. It took lots of "failure" at trying to succeed in the "job market" before I realized how sweet and sensible life is merely by looking in a different direction. Indeed, "failing" in the jobbing world is a difficult psychological occurrence to handle. After all, the jobbing world tells us that our very identity and self-worth are synonymous with the way we "make a living." For those who have a difficult time finding a way to "make a living," it is psychologically stressful indeed. This is especially true for men, who are socialized very strongly to find and succeed in a job identity.

My story is not going to be too similar to anyone else's story. I'm just one, unique example. In addition to revealing my own story, I will present, later in the book, examples of other people's un-jobbing. We're each unique; but, we do all have some things in common. And, I hope the story which follows will provide some perspective from my life experience, and will put in context the ideas I will discuss in subsequent chapters. Those chapters, in turn, should help you in tailoring these ideas to your unique situation.

CHAPTER 2

A BABYBOOMER'S STORY

I grew up in a home that was in many ways quite typical. There was Mom and Pop, two kids, and a dog. Dad was the major "bread winner," while Mom worked, too, not primarily because she seemed to have a burning desire for a career, but because the family "needed" the second income.

During most of my childhood, we lived in a typical three bedroom, one bathroom house—that is, until the "in-thing" became adding another bathroom and an extra room known as a "family room." (I still wonder what living rooms are for now.)

My parents were good parents—very social justice- and education-oriented. There was never any doubt that my brother and I would be going to college, and that we would succeed at finding jobs which would lead to lifelong careers. This was the message—and it was a strong one—handed to us by society at large through our parents. The message was clearly this: "Yes, you should try to be happy and fulfilled, but keep your life focused on your *career*." Perhaps we heard different actual words than that from our parents and teachers; but, each generation of children has been receiving the above message.

UN-JOBBING

Contradictory words make no difference. The cultural message of emphasizing career has been speaking so loudly, that we have not been able to hear any other words.

Unfortunately, as far as the job market was concerned, the "field" I fell in love with was music. For my brother, it was political science and law. Guess which one of us became more "employable"? But I was "flipped out" over classical music on the guitar. I had found my bliss, and I didn't concern myself with what I would "do with it." I just wanted to practice and play the guitar and become as fine a musician as I could.

I graduated from college with a Bachelor of Music degree in guitar performance; still, at that point, I was only marginally concerned with what I would "do with my degree." I knew I needed more "education"—I would have to obtain another credential and at least get a master's degree. So I went to graduate school and two years later had my second piece of paper, a Master of Music degree in guitar performance.

Toward the end of graduate school, the cultural line suddenly hit me: I needed to "face the fact" that I would have to get a job in my "field." *Oops*—with little effort and research, I found out that open jobs in my "field" (college teaching positions in guitar) numbered about five per year *in the country*. (I believe there are fewer now than there were then.) I was too intimidated and scared to try for a performing career. Besides, I wanted a *job*: That means I wanted *employment* which would give me a guaranteed salary and the security of knowing how I would make ends meet. That's what I was raised to desire and what I was expected to pursue.

So, my employment picture was not as secure as that of my brother, who, in the meantime, had graduated from Harvard

Law School. But, I loved music and the guitar, and I was going to try hard to get a job. After I made two or three applications, it became apparent that the universities were hiring people with more experience than I had, being "fresh out of graduate school." So, I had to think about, at least temporarily, something less than that desirable career job. My new wife was in music education, and she was offered a modest teaching job in Kentucky. I could go with her, maybe get some part-time teaching jobs and have a private studio. *Then* I could get "the job."

And that's exactly what happened—the first part, that is. I went with my wife to Kentucky, and almost immediately, three colleges were willing to add me as a part-timer to their teaching staffs, provided they could pay me poorly and offer no fringe benefits. I said to myself, "That's fine. I just need to get a few years experience behind me, and *then* I'll be able to get a 'real' job."

I spent the next eight years putting together part-time guitar teaching jobs and privately teaching, telling myself that I really did work "full-time"—just from many different sources. I reasoned that if I thought of myself as working "full-time," then I could ease the self-inflicted guilt I had manufactured about not really having the one, "full-time" job, which is what I ultimately simply *had* to get. Of course, all the pay from all those part-time sources didn't add up to even half of what a full-time university music faculty member typically made.

To put it bluntly, I felt *BADLY*. The message from the whole of society and my upbringing was that I was not "successful." I was a failure. I didn't have either a full-time business (an idea I disliked greatly) or a full-time job. I kept applying to the handful of openings in my "field" that would come up each year. And I kept coming in second place or lower each time.

In the meantime, my marriage ended rather suddenly in divorce. While this was an emotional shock, it didn't feel like the same kind of failure of achievement that I had been experiencing in the employment arena. A broken heart seemed fixable; and it didn't seem like it was my fault that my wife was leaving me. I didn't blame myself. But, being backed into a corner, unable to achieve a decent career life, seemed unfixable, and something worth feeling guilty about.

However, a little later I met and married a woman who was teaching on the music faculty at the local state-supported university. My personal life became much more satisfying, and this helped make more palatable the fact that my employment life was comprised of several poorly-paid part-time jobs.

After awhile, though, I decided I had had enough of my present employment situation. I finally said no to part-time college faculty exploitation and decided I would join that new breed of people called "career switchers." You know—those who read the book *What Color is Your Parachute?*, etc. Then I would discover other hidden talents beyond playing and teaching the guitar; and *then* I would get one of those full-time, life-time career jobs, complete with all the benefits and the security of knowing that I would have the income to be able to support me and my family. I was determined that, one way or another, I was going to get a full-time, career job with benefits—even if this job was something that had nothing to do with the years of training I had put in thus far in my life.

So, let's see…I had training, experience, and interest in the arts, including arts administration, and writing. Hmm…There were lots of jobs that could use abilities in these areas. But, could I get one? Good question.

Although I tried like crazy, I never got one. There was always one reason or another—usually the reason was that I just didn't have as much "relevant" experience as another applicant. Of course, I had just spent the last twenty years of my life becoming a guitarist. I could only got hired doing "X" if I had just spent several years doing exactly "X" somewhere else. If I were doing other things, but clearly had the ability and even the (albeit "off the record") experience to do "X," I still came in second place or lower in the competition to win a job. I went through an eight-month period of agony, thinking of myself as that dreadful "U-word"—*UNEMPLOYED*.

Soon, I found out about a half-time job as an academic advisor to "undecided" college students. It offered pretty good pay for the hours involved, so I applied for it (what the hey!), and I got it. I could certainly have interesting things to say to career-oriented, undecided college students; and, I could combine this half-time job with free-lance music teaching and performing.

This worked out alright, but I still felt *terrible* about being a job market "failure." I still pined away, and made some applications, for that one full-time, career job complete with a benefits package and security.

During this "advising period," though, I did a great deal of thinking about life and living, and "making a living." I was really big on advising my advisees to do what they loved. I knew about the book *Do What You Love, the Money Will Follow* (see Appendix), and my heart wanted very badly to believe in that. So, what was it that I loved besides music and the guitar?

The answer—I still loved music and the guitar, but I also discovered after much introspection that I was a "closet peacenik." I wanted to bring more peace and justice into the world. A lofty idea; but how could I go about it? I started reading everything I could find on the subject and connecting with local groups working in this arena. I got excited—there appeared to be much to learn and much work to do (job security?).

I went to meetings of the local Council for Peace and Justice, and within only a few months I offered myself as a replacement for their fine, but somewhat burned out, "Executive Director." Now, this "Executive Director" was a part-time employee paid, at the time (please restrain your excitement here), $100 a month. But I was so interested in the work and I was so cynical about ever getting a "real" job, that I jumped at this chance, and they hired me.

I continued in the advising job, but after a while as a newly-out-of-the-closet peace activist, I got the idea that I wanted to work "full-time" in the peace and justice movement. Of course, that's another joke. If there's any "field" with as few full-time jobs in it as college guitar teaching, it was the peace and justice movement. After all, everyone wants peace and justice, but no one seems willing or able to pay for it.

AM I GETTING THE MESSAGE?

Finally, after more reading and connecting with people, and having many heavy discussions with my wife—who was herself getting ready to do the *reverse* of what I had been wracking my brain over for years and *resign from* her "real" job!—my thinking got turned around. For starters, I realized that through all of my poorly-paid employment life, my financial needs had always been met! I had *never* experienced any critical or grave financial difficulties. This was true no matter what my situation had been: whether it was when I was by myself and piecing together part-time work, or when I was living with a spouse who had a full-time job, or when I was living with a spouse who was full-time in school and I still had the several poorly-paid part-time jobs. In *all* those cases, I realized that my true financial needs were never in any real jeopardy. True financial needs are far less than the cultural line leads one to believe. But I also had made many more realizations; and these will be discussed in the rest of this book.

With these new revelations and realizations, my wife and I had gathered enough courage to break out of a very strong cultural mold. We then made a bold, simultaneous double "leap off the cliff": she quit her full-time tenured professorship and I quit my half-time advising job at the same time, effective December 31, 1990. This simultaneously wiped away about $43,000 per year in gross salary, and left us with very little guaranteed income.

Had we lost our senses? Perhaps. But it has turned out that it is more accurate to say we had *come to* our senses. Our discussions with each other and with close friends had given us enough courage to take that leap and then allow ourselves some time to get re-adjusted—to losing our former identities (as a music professor, as an academic advisor, as a whatever job identity), and to gaining truer identities (as a being of love who wishes to share with the community things which I'm good at and which make me happy and joyous). That, dear readers, is a major change in self-identity. And, it's a change in self-identity which makes one see the world in an entirely different way than the conventional view of the world.

And so, after some months, things began to work out. My turned around thinking was saying that maybe, just maybe, I didn't want a full-time job in the first place! Coming out of this culture— and especially as a man—that's a shocking idea! My new thinking was saying that maybe it's a *blessing*, after all those years of beating my head against the wall of full-time jobs, that I never *got* a full-time job! Maybe, just maybe, there's a better life besides one dominated by, and pre-occupied with, "making a living"! Maybe, we're here on Earth for better purposes than "making a living."

I now think there are no maybes about it. I'm now convinced that I don't want, and wonderfully happy that I don't have, a single, full-time, lifelong career type of job. And I can't even imagine an offer that would entice me to take such a job now, even if someone were to put one right in my lap! There are joys and life-changing realizations that I now experience that I had no inkling about until I stepped off the job-dominated merry-go-round. Even someone like myself, who never actually *held* a single, full-time career-type job, can still very much be on that merry-go-round. I was definitely on it, merely by my buying into that cultural message. Other people have come to this perspective, as I have not, after being very "successful" in the "jobbing" world. It makes no difference. The main point of this book is not really about money, and how we "support" ourselves. I don't wish to belittle the importance of understanding money, and having a good relationship with money. Definitely, money plays a major part in the focus of this book. But, the most important point is to question and carefully reflect upon how we are *spending our lives*. Money is secondary to life.

Chapter by chapter, I'll be giving you the details of why I'm so convinced that a home-based, non-job-dominated life is one I wouldn't trade for the old way. In addition, I'll offer tools, ideas, and suggestions on how to live such a life.

The next chapter offers a little crash course in the history of labor—especially the recent, incredibly fast-changing progression of society's concept of what it means to be "making a living."

CHAPTER 3

ABOUT "MAKING A LIVING"

What I realized, as a result of the life experiences I recounted in the previous chapter, is that the idea of "making a living" has gotten way out of hand. People in our society at the close of the twentieth century consider the idea that one needs to "make a living" to be normal and natural. As economist Henry George tried to warn us over a century ago in his monumental work *Progress and Poverty*, "What more than anything else prevents the realization of...injustice...is that mental habit which makes anything that has long existed seem natural and necessary." "Making a living" has become normal (i.e. the norm), but our present society's expectation of us to "make a living" is far from natural or necessary when one examines "making a living" from both an historical and personal point of view. But, because we have been steeped in the "making a living" institution for all of our lives and the lives of our parents and their parents, we are deluded into thinking that "making a living" is natural and necessary.

First, let's look at the progression of labor history a little bit. It's an interesting story—

UN-JOBBING

HOW WE GOT WHERE WE ARE TODAY

Once upon a time, we humans began inhabiting this planet. At first, the major issues for people were how to eat and how to stay warm; and hunter/gatherer societies came into being. But it is difficult, and even rather humorous, to imagine that the people of those early times spent most of their awake hours working for food and clothing.

Indeed, it would seem logical that, even from earliest times, humans had recreational, leisure, artistic, and various communal activities. Many of these activities may have been a great deal more "sophisticated" than many of us modern humans would like to admit.

Gradually, agricultural knowledge grew, and societies became more organized about food procurement. But, even at this point, people worked to "put food on the table" only as much as necessary.

As history marched on, however, the idea began to take hold that a person could grow food and/or make things beyond what his family needed and sell (or barter) the excess for something another person had. At this point there was not yet the concept of what we, today, would call "making a living." This was a more loosely organized lifestyle of taking care of one's own needs while doing some modest amount of selling/bartering. Still, no doubt, these people had rich recreational/cultural/communal lives. This is what basically went on for centuries.

In fact, for 99 percent of the time that humans have inhabited the Earth, people have lived communally, in tribes and villages. The kind of life that we take for granted and is normal today—big cities where adults and children leave their single-family homesteads all day for working (or schooling) in large institutional settings—is only a *very* recent phenomenon. This has been the case for less than one percent of the time humans have inhabited Earth.

THE PICTURE CHANGES

And then, less than two centuries ago, the Industrial Revolution arrived. Operating the new machinery of mass production provided jobs and income to a new class of consumers while making consumer goods plentiful. Now, in an historically-sudden occurrence, people (usually men) began to identify the time they spent laboring for mass production as their "work" time. Bartering was fading away and selling became the main way of doing business. With more cash in people's pockets, there was money to buy necessities—food, clothing, and shelter—along with an extra amount for all the new machines being mass produced.

Even children got into this act; and, in spite of child labor laws it wasn't until government compulsory schooling came about that children were not a significant part of "making a living." However, this merely transferred children from one unnatural confinement to another. It is not commonly realized that public school came about not just for education purposes, but because children needed a place to go and exist while their parents were working in Industrial Revolution factories. Before the Industrial Revolution, there didn't seem to be the pressing need for school. After all, parents and other adults were available to children; and they were learning just fine (in fact, many would say better than school children are today). And, the important thing about this, in this "making a living" kind of thinking, was that public schooling "created" a whole new category of jobs in the field of education—teachers, principals, janitors, cafeteria workers, bus drivers, administrators. (For very insightful writing on this see *Dumbing Us Down* by John Taylor Gatto, listed in the Appendix, and any of the many books by John Holt.)

But, back to our story. People were working at a frantic pace. The result: a greater amount of goods were produced and, at the same time, people were making more money to buy these larger inventories of goods. So, in an historically-sudden moment, people (mostly men) began "making a living"— defined as: *that singular, full-day activity which one does in order to earn the money to buy the results of what other people do to "make a living."* People had earned money with their "trades" for quite some time, but the difference between this time and earlier is that now "work" time became more organized, structured, and regimented. It became the major aspect of people's lives and *clearly distinct from* their non-"work" lives. The idea of a job in the context of the Industrial Revolution turned meaningful work into merely an "occupation" with a paycheck.

CAN WE PUT THE BRAKES ON THIS?

There was some sentiment to calm down this working frenzy and a 40-hour work week was brought about. People reasoned that there was ample time to have a life of culture, leisure, and communion with the time that was outside of one's 40-hour per week job.

The "modernization" continued, however, and the inventions began to be more sophisticated, more costly, and produced more quickly. The result: more "desirable," expensive goods were available in greater quantities than ever before.

This put great pressure on the man (the one "making a living") to work more to meet his family's "needs." There was pressure to expand the work week again, and the concept of overtime came into being. In additon, women were obtaining new "rights," and that half of the population began to be seen as potential "workers" to help in the cause of "making a living." Those families with either two wage earners or one willing to work beyond the 40-hour week managed pretty well at this point. Keep in mind that all of this is happening, historically speaking, *very* quickly. And, the "modernization," industrially speaking, was continuing at a frantic pace.

A major addition to this picture was the impact of war-making in this century. This century has seen more wars than probably any other in history (including "pre-history"). There were two important effects of this on the world of labor: war-making and war-preparation became (1) a major category of manufacturing of the Industrial Revolution, and (2) an extremely expensive fact of life, since the weapons cost a lot more than they used to. What did this mean for those "making a living"?

Enter the income tax, an idea which was created to pay for the high cost of war-making. Many people do not realize that, were it not for wars and the preparations for wars, the income tax might not ever have been created. Wage earners, under the income tax, now needed to earn a much higher "gross" income in order to net what they were used to making prior to the income tax. Because of that, there was pressure on salaries to go up, which meant that goods and services started to cost more, which meant that there became more pressure to keep salaries going up...etc. and etc. This was not the invention, but it certainly was the quintessential demonstration, of what inflation is all about. (The income tax, by the way, had been around for some time, but prior to this time only the very richest of people—the top 1% or so—were affected at all. For more discussion on taxes, see Chapter VII.)

The history of post-World Wars United States is quite familiar to us. By the 1980s, two wage earners (each working more hours) were not "doing as well" as one wage earner had done as recently as the 1920s.

OK, so much for an admittedly simplified, non-scholarly, crash summary of the history of labor. But, what about the personal aspects of "making a living"?

WHAT THIS REALLY MEANS

The Industrial Revolution convinced the society that one could have, in effect, *two distinct lives*—(1) the "work" life and (2) the life outside of one's job. Society convinced workers that their "work" life was something that they may or may not have chosen to do if they didn't "need" the money to buy the things that suddenly seemed necessary. It became acceptable, even common, that "work" was something one didn't necessarily like all that much, but had to be tolerated. Oh well, society thought, one has to "make a living."

Yet, somehow, the thought of questioning why people spent such a huge portion of their lives in an activity that they would not have chosen to do if they were to take money out of the picture just didn't happen. Indeed, at this point, there is so much agreement on the need to "make a living," that this concept goes virtually unquestioned by the vast majority of people in our culture. Yet, 40, 50, 60 or more hours per week are spent at "work" by people, the vast majority of whom would quit at the drop of a hat if someone were just to give them their salary. People are spending so much of their days, their weeks—indeed their lives—"making a living," that a good portion of their remaining time, their other ever shrinking life, is spent recuperating and vacating (hence, the "vacation") from their "making a living." In fact, many people "make their living" in the business of helping people recuperate and vacate from their "making a living."

Joe Dominguez has more accurately tagged this concept "making a dying." (Dominguez started a non-profit organization to help people in understanding these things. I am indebted to them, The New Road Map Foundation, for their work which has helped me tremendously. See Appendix for contact information.) As I reflect on the history above, I see his point. In less than a couple of centuries—a mere *blink* in the span of human inhabitation on Earth—"work" became organized (as well as pressured by people "making their living" in the advertising industry creating false "needs") to the point of removing one's true life from one's life. Hence, it could be more accurately called "making a dying."

UN-JOBBING

Indeed, the pressure we have put on those "making a living" has been relentless and steadily increasing. For an example, take the automobile. In the years just after the automobile was invented, few people owned one. But very gradually, nearly every household acquired one. Now practically each person past the age of 16 has one. And, since "making a living" causes us to be more away from home, automobiles have become fancier in order to be that "home away from home." Of course, that means they cost a lot more, which means we have to "work" more...etc. and etc. This is a typical example of the multi-spiral situation we are in. It has gotten way out of hand.

I, like many of you I'm sure, have reflected on that age-old philosophical question of why we humans are here on Earth. My answer is certainly *not* to "make a living." What we *are* here for can only be answered truly by each individual. For me, it involves loving and caring for one another (which, at least to some extent, involves being with one another in social and other *cooperative*, rather than competitive, situations), and creating our lives according to our gifts, not according to how we think we can obtain money.

Perhaps that—creating our lives according to our gifts— is what I could properly call making a living—without the quotation marks. In other words, instead of being dominated by "making a living," we should be oriented around making our lives. Whatever you feel you are here for, does it not strike you as more than odd that adults leave the house all day "making a living" while the kids leave the house all day being prepared for the day when they will be "making a living?" Then everyone comes home at the end of the quasi-interesting, quasi-boring day, hurries through an evening, and gets up the next morning to leave the house and do the same thing. And, we do this for the bulk of our able-bodied years on this Earth. A great many people don't like all that much how they spend all this time; and what they do during all this time is often not very sustainable or healthy for themselves or for the planet. I ask you: *where is life?*

You may be thinking that these ideas are all fine and good, and it's alright if a few people here and there do this kind of thing, but what if everybody did un-jobbing? Wouldn't that wreak too much havoc on things? Where would our comforts and security come from?

REDEFINING WEALTH

What we have to realize is that there are all kinds of wealth, and our current way of defining wealth is just one, historically very recent, way. What we need, in the words of author Daniel Quinn, is an economy based on *support* instead of *products*. Right now, we have an economy based on making products and getting products. And, our way of defining wealth has to do with making more money and accumulating more things, and then making more money and accumulating more things. We're caught in the vicious circle involving products which merely goes round and round while it increasingly threatens the quality of our lives and our environment. Even services are "productized" in our way of doing things.

Instead, if we look at societies not based on our way of economics, we see a different economy. And, it *is* an economy. Quinn calls these societies "Leaver" societies. Modern industrial societies are "Taker" societies. (For more on this see Quinn's book *Ishmael* listed in the Appendix.)

In Leaver societies, we see an economy based on giving support and getting support. People in these societies don't do this because they are necessarily more compassionate than we are. They do it because this is how they create their security, their "wealth." In these sorts of societies, everyone contributes to the common good, everyone "works" at something that is utilizing his or her gifts, and everyone is taken care of. No one goes hungry or without "health care" or without shelter or love. And, no one has a life without true meaning or freedom. It's a true safety net; and everyone is a part of it, and everyone benefits from it. This kind of society is true wealth, no one "falls through the cracks," and it's much easier on the environment! And, it's one that still exists in small hidden corners of the planet right now. It's also one that has, to a greater extent than now, existed for humans all over the planet for 99 percent of the time we humans have been on Earth. What else could we ask for?

Of course, not all societies in earlier times took care of everyone equally. But, such "Leaver" societies were much more often the case before the Industrial Revolution than they are now. We can't all go back to living in an indigenous tribe. But, it is possible to create in modern society a way of life which is much more "Leaver" in nature than what we have now. Obviously, this will take a different way of looking at life and our self-identities.

This question of how we spend the bulk of our waking hours—and why—may be new to some. And it may seem like there are no alternatives to the answers our society strongly suggests. But when we consider the consequences of those answers from contemporary society, we realize that such matters as personal fulfillment and social and environmental costs are usually lost in the predominant concern about jobs and a "growth economy."

Would we stay in our jobs if we did not need the salary? That question is an excellent exercise to answer truthfully for oneself. I urge you to ask yourself that question very seriously. Does your work make the world a better place in which to live? Does your work fulfill your purpose for being alive here on Earth? If the answers to those questions are "no," then, most importantly, are there alternatives?

To arrive at some alternative answers, let's continue by taking a different view, and a more detailed look, at the "science" of economics.

CHAPTER 4

A DIFFERENT VIEW OF ECONOMICS

Recall practically any recent Presidential election year, and you'll remember that talk about jobs was everywhere. "Jobs, jobs, jobs" always dominates the plaints of the voters and the promises of the politicians. Almost everyone calls for consumer spending to pick up, "creating" more jobs in both manufacturing and marketing. And almost everyone calls for the government to help—even if it means spending beyond its means and going deeper into debt—in order to "fix" our ailing economy. I believe this approach is wrong, and that we need a radical rethinking of economics in this country and the world: buying *less*—with *less* emphasis on jobs—is what we need, not buying more.

What I'm talking about is changing our way of economically relating to one another from *competition* to *cooperation*. We are living in a culture which claims that competition is just "human nature," that we just can't help it when we destroy each other or when we continue to widen the gap between the rich and the poor. Personally, I believe that it is just as much "human nature" to help another and share with another than to try to defeat—economically or otherwise—another. Regardless of your view of "human nature," most people would agree that people can *learn* to act either cooperatively or competitively. I think we should choose to act cooperatively, because by now it's painfully obvious what our competitive ways are doing. Just look at where we have put ourselves by operating in terms of competition and "growth economics":

THE FALLACY OF "GROWTH IS GOOD"

Principally, we've been caught in a destructive cycle of alternating boom and bust—"good times" and "recession"—that merely keeps going round and round. As world population increases—it is now at around five and a half billion—the Earth will be crying out louder and louder that ever increasing buying and consuming and competing are doing us in. Not only does the Earth suffer from this kind of thinking, but so do most, if not all, societies, for in a competitive world where social welfare is defined as the ability to consume, there are always some people or nations who have the upper hand and others who have the lower hand. And, even though some of us may be "winners" and some "losers" in this way of approaching life, all of us are on the same sinking ship. In other words, in long-term large perspective thinking, we will either be (from an economic standpoint) all winners or all losers. Right now, we're all losers.

Think about this for a minute. Suppose you sell "X's" and the demand is picking up. ("X's" could be a product or a service.) Eventually people are going to spend so much money on "X's" that they will have to stop buying them because they are cash poor and/or they are suffering under a mountain of debt and/or they just don't need any more "X's" right now. This brings about what is called a "recession," because the demand for "X's" is less, and consequently fewer people are needed to make and sell them. As a result, some people lose their jobs. Everyone cries out: "We've got to get our economy going again, 'create' jobs, and be able to compete in the world!" Eventually, people find themselves with more spending money again (because their personal spending has gone down) and they start buying more "X's," which "creates" more jobs for people making and selling "X's." OK—now you can start reading again at "Suppose you sell 'X's'" and put yourself in a continuous loop. And you can go around and around and around the loop, ad infinitum.

But why are we in this crazy continuous loop?

WHAT IS A "HEALTHY" ECONOMY?

It's time to stop measuring our economic health by how many cars, toasters, sweaters, etc. that people are buying. This is the classic example of being "penny wise, but pound foolish." This way of measuring economic health also gives us the amazing "facts" that the oil spills and hurricanes are "good" for the economy, because they "create jobs" in the clean-up. We're now hooked on something aptly called the Gross Domestic Product. All the GDP cares about is how much money people are making and then spending. It has no consciousness about what effect those products or services are having on the planet or on people and their lives. The making of some product could be destroying the environment or causing high rates of cancer in a group of people or just generally stressing out and wasting their lifetimes. It doesn't matter. All the GDP cares about is that people are making and spending a lot of money. But it's time we kept in mind the long-term sustainability of the planet and the well-being and personal fulfillment of its inhabitants when measuring the "health" of our economy. Why should the entire "science" of economics be devoid of *consciousness*?

We must keep in mind that every material good—no matter how useful we think it is—is an extraction from the planet. With the US leading the way with its overly consumptive way of life, we are straining the Earth. We exist in a competitive, dog-eat-dog world divided into "winners" and "losers;" and, the dividing line between the two categories is constantly moving. Inevitably, some people who are "winners" now, become "losers" later—and vice versa. This is the way—by definition—competition is. Competition involves—by definition—a *defeat* of somebody. If our way of life is economic competition, then some people, by definition, lose out. For me, that means we all lose. When I hear our politicians crying out for us to be more "competitive," it makes me cringe.

Any way you look at it, competition is at best a win-lose situation, with people hoping and praying that *they* will not be on the losing end of the stick. And that is in the short term. In the long term, it is a total lose-lose situation for the planet and the life on it. (For very insightful, well-researched writing on this, see *No Contest—The Case Against Competition: Why We Lose in our Race to Win* by Alfie Kohn. Even the most diehard believer in competition being a part of "human nature" will have plenty of food for thought with this myth-shattering book.

A DIFFERENT VIEW OF ECONOMICS

I'm convinced that we don't need to be competitive. We can *choose* to be, but it is not necessary by our "nature." See appendix.) In short, the only true way to help our situation is to come up with a "win-win" lifestyle.

How can we get *everyone* to win? It's simple, yet extremely difficult. All we have to do is base all our thinking and actions on a foundation of caring for the planet and concern for the *quality* of the life on it: change competition to cooperation and sharing, and, in addition, stop calling for the government to bail us out with "job creation," or, for that matter, putting any stock into *believing* in "job creation." The US government is a great financial fiasco. It has amassed an unconscionable debt, spends huge amounts on war-preparations and war-making, and has programs in agriculture and energy which contribute to the poisoning of the planet. It's difficult for me to imagine at this point that this institution could somehow create a society in which all people are economically secure, much less a society in which all people have true freedom to pursue their own joys and gifts.

More and more, it is obvious to me that the government is not the answer to our economic woes. Governments do have their good purposes—fire departments, mass transit, libraries, parks and recreation programs to name a few—but, aside from these kinds of things, the government is a major part of the problem with our economy because of its bloated size, "growth" and competition philosophy, and largely irresponsible spending habits. It cannot be part of the solution, except by not being part of the problem. Large, out of control, competition-driven bureaucracies are not the answer. *We* are the answer. You and I. And the answer is and must be: We can change our world by changing ourselves.

GETTING OFF THE COMPETITION MERRY-GO-ROUND

How can we step off this cycle and change this situation? As an important first, giant step, we can change our view about economics. Particularly, when we hear that consumer spending is down, when we hear that housing starts are down, when we hear that the automobile industry is sluggish, *we should jump for joy! THAT'S GOOD!!* In those times, we're being less wasteful and more ecologically responsible; it is more likely that, in this type of economic situation, people are learning more about what truly counts in life.

We *can* make great changes, but it's our actions which speak much louder than our words. Indeed, changes in our lives—in how we live—can more easily make for changes in our thinking than the other way around. In the remaining chapters of this book, I will go into all sorts of ways we can contribute, by our actions, to this new type of economics. It involves answering the question: how much is enough? It's a whole, different way of looking at the world—like the title of the 1970s economics classic *Small is Beautiful* by E. F. Schumacher (see Appendix). This new way of looking at the world involves acting more on a small, human scale than on a large, centralized, massively institutionalized scale.

We are told that the world is "shrinking" and that we live in a kind of "global village." Of course, in spite of the technologies of instant communication, the world is not really shrinking; but. it is getting more and more crowded all the time. Instead of considering ourselves in a *global village*, where shipping goods over thousands of miles is more normal than neighbors helping one another, we should be thinking in terms of a *globe of villages*—lots of small-scale, localized, self-reliant communities. It is so much easier for people to take care of one another when it is in the context of a small-scale, personal community. Massive, largely centralized systems get bogged down in a bureaucracy that is expensive, highly impersonal, ineffective, and competition-oriented. We need to think of more localized designs of support systems. There are people and communities who are already living and working in this way of economically relating, even within western societies. Information and experience is already out there. (Lots of ideas can be found on this from organizations and books listed in the Appendix.) But, most of us are too busy spending our lives in the competitive job market either to have the time (or energy) to move in this direction or to notice that another way even exists.

We also need to ask some probing questions about very common assumptions we have.

Take one prime example: why should some people spend their entire lives depending on how much money other people spend on cars? The product of this very competitive industry has done many things to our planet: the Earth is polluted with the detritus of worn-out cars and parts of cars and is increasingly covered with asphalt; the planet's air is almost unbreathable in places by millions who are, by the nature of the urban sprawl made possible by the auto, forced to spend a large part of their income—and therefore a large part of their productive lives in the pursuit of money with which to buy, operate, and maintain a car—in order to have a ticket into this whole unfortunate system. The negatives which surface from honestly and thoroughly answering such questions as "Why should some people spend their entire lives depending on how much money other people spend on cars?" to me far outweigh what seems to be a positive—that a group of people are able to "make a living." Clearly, "growth" in the automobile industry is not good when viewed from a larger picture, a picture that goes beyond the fact that people can "make their living" from it.

CAN WE CHANGE THE ECONOMY?

Change can be difficult. When things are really messed up, there can be pain in the effort to come clean. But giving up the so-called "American Dream" (which has always been penny-wise and pound-foolish) is well worth the trade-off for living in a world in which people are cooperating and harmonizing and acting in an ecologically responsible way. This materialistic "American Dream" is something we need to wake up from. I believe this is a case of "we can never get enough of what we really didn't want in the first place." We can help each other in many ways in this transition effort. Indeed, a change to a more cooperative view of economics can actually be a *rewarding* process because it would increase our experience of real community.

One thing we can do in the effort to change the economy is organize, join, and actively participate in more co-ops of all kinds. Co-ops and credit unions are based on the principles of democracy in decision-making and justice in the equitable distribution of benefits. By creating more cooperatives, strengthening more of the existing ones, and transforming non-cooperative organizations into cooperative ones, it is conceivable that we could change our current global competitive society into a global cooperative society. This is admittedly very long-term, but the co-op blueprint already exists and is operating throughout the world. (See appendix for information about an organization with this very mission called, appropriately, The Global Cooperative Society.)

In addition, we can conduct our individual lives more cooperatively. And, when our consuming naturally goes down, we will have less *need* for money in the first place and we won't be so imprisoned by the institution of "making a living." In this way, we can spend more of our lives truly *living*, rather than "making a living" and be much happier and more fulfilled. In my mind, this is true prosperity. Indeed, in a world such as this, there would be no such thing as a "recession." And, all times, economically speaking, would be "good times."

But, trying to continue to be the number one nation with high spending, high wages, high debt, and high ecological destruction is taking us in the wrong direction. It's time to embrace the infiniteness of the world of unity, sharing, and love which comes about by seeing the other person (or nation) not as another "dog" in competition with us for more things, but as a person (or nation) with intrinsic worth who can help us and receive our help.

Cranking up our current system more may end this or that "recession," but it will only sink our ship a little deeper as we merrily consume our way around and around in the continuous loop of "good" and "bad" economic times.

Again, jobs aren't really "created," they're bought. And the more all of us are buying each other's jobs, the more income we need to make in our own jobs, which in turn necessitates more buying of others' jobs, which in turn... This stuff can only take us to higher and higher stakes, spelling greater and greater disaster. Not participating in this competitive upwardly spiraling consumerism (as much as possible) by an individual would be a great favor to the whole world as well as to the individual.

I say let's step off this crazy, environmentally destructive continuous loop. The next step? At this point, it would be helpful to assess the *costs* of your current life, and what your true needs actually are.

In addition, we can learn to let go of our fear about how we are going to pay for our necessities. This is not easy, and I don't wish to make light of this; but it can be done. A support group of friends is extremely helpful. Fear, I have found, is always self-manufactured, and it's possible to spend years worrying about this without realizing that things have worked out pretty well in spite of the worry. Let's remind ourselves, too, that there are different ways of looking at the world and assessing what our true needs are, than what we get from the daily newspaper or the evening TV news and all the commercialism therein. (I'll have more to say on that later.)

With those thoughts in mind, it's time to start getting specific to your situation. Before you assess your needs, let's take a look at this question: How much is your job *costing* you?

CHAPTER 5

HOW MUCH IS YOUR JOB *COSTING* YOU?

Some readers may be responding to the above chapter title with a puzzled, "Wait a minute. *Costing* me? I think of my job as the way I *make* money."

Right. It *is* the way you make money; but your job also costs you a great deal of money. It's so taken for granted and assumed that we have to have regular, major income-producing employment, that we are willing to put up with all kinds of strains and drains on our lives due to our jobs. But make no mistake here, there are plenty of costs—monetary and otherwise—to having a job.

I've already more than hinted at the time (or rather *life*) costs of having a regular, full-time job: 9 to 5 till 65, week after week, year after year, for the bulk of one's able-bodied life, doing something which may have at least questionable environmental impact, and which may be only mildly interesting. Those costs alone are enough to justify the main point of this chapter—that jobs may not be worth the various prices we pay.

But let's consider for the moment just the *financial* costs of most kinds of employment.

Indulge me here, if you will. Imagine you've been living in some "fairyland" in which you've not needed to make any income; you've just been existing in a blissful, totally joyous state without any of the regular, worldly issues of running an earthly, human life. You have had no financial needs. Everything has been taken care of.

Now—imagine that somehow you've lost the magic which gave you such a life void of any financial concerns whatsoever. The only good thing about being rudely snapped out of your heavenly, worry-free existence is that, somehow, the Universe did manage to get you a job so that you can "make ends meet" now that you have to concern yourself with financial matters.

You now have a job with the Framapplicator Co. which will require you to report to a building some 5 or 6 miles from your house and work Monday through Friday. You will need to arrive at the office by 8:30 or 9:00 a.m. each morning and will not leave the office before 5:00 p.m. The job will also require some longer days and some weekends, depending on the projects and deadlines at hand. You will also have some travel out of town from time to time.

With those assumptions in mind, consider the financial burdens this job puts on you. Remember, we're not speaking at all about the life energy burdens, just the financial burdens.

HERE COMES SOME HOMEWORK

YOUR CAR. Without the job, you might not have even needed a car. Even if you had one, you're certainly going to be driving it a great deal more now. Current estimates place the cost of driving a car at 30 cents per mile. At ten miles round trip per day (to use a typical round figure) times five trips per week times forty-eight weeks a year (allowing a generous four-week vacation), the result is $720 of job-related car expense per year. You may also have job-related parking costs. Perhaps you even "need" to have a certain class, size, or quality of car because of your job, a more expensive car (to buy, to drive, to service and maintain, to insure, etc.) than you would have if you didn't have your job. The 30 cents a mile figure is an average figure; so, if you're driving a higher priced car, your costs per mile would be higher. Perhaps, your family could easily have just one car instead of two or more, if no one had a job away from home. That would be a considerable expense saved. With only one car, for example, you'd have only one car insurance policy instead of two or more.

CHILDCARE. If you have to pay for childcare because of your job, you get a tax credit, but keep in mind a couple of things: (1) even with that small credit in April, you still have to pay for childcare each week as it comes, and (2) the more "successful" you are at your job (i.e. the more money you make), the less tax credit you get. As an example, one year I had childcare expenses in excess of $2400 for one child, and received a tax credit of only $280. So, it's fair to say that each child completely eats up the $2,000 or so "allowance" on your income tax return if you have full-time childcare to pay for. This tax return "allowance" is something you would still have without your job and without childcare to pay.

And speaking of TAXES. I'll be going into much more

thought and detail about taxes a couple of chapters from now. But at this point, think about the amount of money you send to federal, state, and local governments which is siphoned off your paycheck. This is *your* money I'm talking about. The withholding from paychecks is so ingrained now that people don't even consider that their "gross" pay is their salary. People actually consider their "net" pay to be their salary, because they never see the difference. Yet your full "gross" salary is actually money your employer paid you for the job you do.

How much is your withheld money? And, if you haven't done so already, consider how much you are spending here and what that money is being used for, and what that does to the planet and its inhabitants. This is money you have earned *and are spending* because of your job. Taxes are neither certain nor something completely out of our control. There is much you can do to get your taxpaying in alignment with your values. See Chapter VII.

Keep in mind that many times the addition of a small amount of income into a family can bring the income into a higher tax bracket, which can take a serious bite out of what appears to be "extra" income. Often a second income in a household is much more costly than the first as far as taxes are concerned. Check out the book *Two Incomes and Still Broke?* by Linda Kelley (see Appendix).

FOOD. Consider for yourself how much money you spend on lunches because of your job, balancing that figure with how much you would spend on eating lunch if you were home because you didn't have that job. Also, consider the money you spend on eating dinner out, because you are too tired from your job all day to cook when you get home. Or, consider the money you spend on quick, convenience foods, also because you are too tired from working at your job all day to cook when you get home. Figuring this may seem tricky. But, try to think what you did in this regard over a typical one month period, add it up, and multiply that by 12 to get an approximate yearly figure. Being tired from our stressful jobs can translate into a great deal of monetary expense in many areas of our lives.

CLOTHING. Take a good look in your dresser and in your closets and try to figure some sort of yearly estimate of what you spend on clothes you would not buy were it not for your job. If you are in the "white collar" world this could be considerable. Remember to figure in the specialized dry cleaning of your job clothing.

MEDICAL SERVICES. Even if you have health insurance paid for by your employer, you may incur job-related medical expenses. These may have to do with treatment for job-related psychological stress or job-related physical injury. Even with paid health insurance, you still probably have deductibles, co-payments, and—no surprise to anyone—things which just aren't covered by insurance. Go back over a year's medical history and see what job-related medical expenses you had.

TIMESAVERS. Full-time workers use a variety of strategies to save time because their jobs are very time-consuming. Unfortuanately, these "timesavers" cost money. Perhaps you hire work or cleaning done around the house that you could do yourself but you're too busy because of your job. There may be machines that you have bought to save time that you wouldn't have bought if you didn't have your time taken up with your job. In addition, when you shop for items, you may not have taken the time to make price comparisons, because you were too tied up with your job. And so, you end up paying more for an item than you might have paid if you didn't have your job and had more time to research.

All of these things are difficult to quantify. It seems subtle, because these timesavers are such a "normal" part of modern life. Very quietly, though, timesavers—done because of your job—are costing you money.

MISCELLANEOUS. A lot of job-related expenses, especially if they begin to seem part of your home routine, are easy to overlook. Perhaps you make some long distance business calls from home. Maybe there are pet care expenses because of your job (like kennel expenses when you go out of town on business). Go back through an old calendar of yours, and look at everything you did. If something was done because of your job, estimate an expense. Add it up.

By now you see the point. A full-time job is a two-edged sword, even just financially speaking. It has both an asset and a liability side to its equation. Yes, you end up making a "profit" at your job (in most cases), but a job does not represent all "profit" by any means. There is much about the spend-your-lifetime-in-a-full-time-job lifestyle which costs you a significant amount of money. Most people don't realize that many of their everyday expenses, which have become so commonplace that they are taken for granted, only exist because of employment.

I know that there is potentially a lot of "homework" suggested in this chapter. But, it is important to get a good handle on the costs—financial and otherwise—of your employment life. This is important and useful information. You can use this information with recommendations I will give later in this book.

If you want more help with estimating the financial costs of your job, I'll recommend again the book called *Two Incomes and Still Broke?* by Linda Kelley (see Appendix).

UNDERSTANDING THIS VICIOUS CIRCLE

When I was a university academic advisor, many students complained to me that they couldn't do their school work because of a lack of time. We would then have a conversation that would go something like this:

"Why are you short on time?" I would ask.

"Because I have to work too many hours a week," the student would say.

"Why do you have to work so much?"

"Well, my car is very expensive. I have payments to make; and the gas, repairs, and insurance are killing me."

"Why do you even need a car as a college student?" I would reply.

"Well, I have to have some way to get to work," came the answer.

UN-JOBBING

Usually the student literally couldn't see the vicious circle he or she had just described, even right after having the above conversation. Interestingly, the student's car was quite often a "nicer" one than mine. This typical conversation describes the situation in which many of us past "school-age" are finding ourselves also: We need our jobs, to some extent, to make money for the things which cost money because of our jobs. This is another crazy, continuous loop.

In fact, there is a growing trend among two wage-earner couples in the United States right now. Many of these couples are discovering that the spouse with the "second income" is typically spending (for clothing, transportation, meals, childcare, timesavers, higher tax bracket. etc.) as much money—and sometimes more—*because* of the job than he or she is making *from* the job. Shocking as it may seem, a "second income" can actually be a money *loser*. When such a discovery is made, quite often this person, realizing that the family cannot *afford* this job, rather quickly quits the job. It's amazing: when push comes to shove, and someone proves that a job is not really producing a net income, or at least a net income of any significance, then quickly the person sees no need for the job. It's quite obvious that the person was in the job solely because he or she thought (falsely) that it made money for the family. There is not enough genuine interest in the job in terms of what it is and the time it consumes to keep the person wanting to stay employed. That is most telling. This is a major example of the value of determining how much a job is costing.

And, again, all of this financial figuring is not even considering what the effect of the job is on a person's *life*. So, if you will, go back and re-read the third paragraph of this chapter. If you couple the *monetary* costs with your *life energy* costs, indeed it's well worth the effort to take stock and deeply consider the question: how much is your job costing you?

Yes, we all need to have some income in order to live in our society. Only those in completely indigenous, non-technological societies can exist without the commodity of money. And, I will have some examples of how un-jobbed people are making money later in this book. The main point for now is that understanding the financial costs of your employment is a very helpful thing because after you've done this "homework," you will likely be able to reduce those financial costs of your employment. By doing that, what income you do make will seem greater, because you will be keeping more of it. This is, in effect, like getting a raise without actually having a higher income. You may even be able to change your employment picture either to another more relaxed situation or to some sort of un-jobbed, self-employment, which could *greatly* reduce the financial costs of your income-producing activity. And that is really the main point of asking the question "how much is your job costing you?" Keep in mind that this is still not touching the area of considering what the activity is that is income-producing. Is it fulfilling your purpose for being alive on Earth? Would you be doing it if financial need were out of the picture? These kinds of questions are important to keep in mind and address.

In the next chapter, we'll consider your entire financial life as that "two-edged sword" with two sides to the equation. The central question is: what would be better—higher income or lower expenses?

CHAPTER 6

WHAT WOULD BE BETTER: HIGHER INCOME OR LOWER EXPENSES?

What do you think? I consider lower expenses to be far more desirable than higher income. This chapter will examine why I think this is so, and then, with that philosophy in mind, how one goes about reducing expenses without feeling deprived.

Your answer to the above question may be that you want *both* higher income and lower expenses. But, I believe that our society is so oriented around gaining more and more income, progressing in this direction throughout one's "career life," that any real focus on lessening expenses gets lost. Our thinking usually gets dominated by the more income side of the equation; and that, more often than not, leads to more stress and dissatisfaction in our lives. So, for the sake of argument and seeing this issue more clearly, let's consider the question as an either/or proposition.

First, consider two hypothetical situations. In the first situation, a person brings home a net income of $1000 a month and has monthly expenses of about $900. In the second case, a person brings in $2500 a month in net income, but has about

$2250 in expenses. Which one of these people would you rather be?

Keep in mind that both of these people are in relatively comfortable financial shape in the sense that both are taking in more money than they are spending (more than we can say for the US government). But I contend that in all ways the person who has the smaller amount of income and expenses is more likely to be the happier, more liberated person, the one who could more easily exercise freedom with time, and the one who could more easily live an ecologically responsible life.

In fact, I've turned around my thinking about the two-sided equation of income and expenses. I see now that people are trapped in a vicious circle. Most people think of life as a constant challenge of meeting expenses, and therefore they focus on the idea of getting/keeping a job (and life-long career) with an ever increasing salary. As a result, more and more of such a person's time is consumed with earning money to constantly chase after and keep up with ever increasing expenses, which we often erroneously equate with "needs."

THE CENTRAL REVELATION OF UN-JOBBING

There is another way of looking at this which seems much more sensible to me: instead of finding ways to meet ever increasing expenses, first I see how many of those expenses can be eliminated or reduced (without feeling like I'm sacrificing, of course); then those reduced or eliminated dollars represent "jobbing" I do not have to do! If I've reduced the amount of "jobbing" in my life, then I'm doing more real *living*, rather than doing the quasi-interesting, quasi-boring "making a living." Stated another way—

The more you can lower your expenses, the more freedom you will have to be the person you truly want to be.

I invite you to re-read the above sentence several times very slowly to allow the words to sink in. I'm talking about your life, and how much freedom you have to spend your life in the way that is most satisfying to you. What could be more important than that?

To clarify this further, it would be helpful to delve into the subject of money and our relationship to it.

MONEY: THE HUSH HUSH TOPIC

Money is a funny and strange thing. Just the mention of it in our culture causes whispers. I'm sure you've noticed this. There are few of us who do not participate in this cultural hush hush attitude toward money. People are more private about how much money they have and earn than just about any other subject, including sex and religion. I'm finding this kind of approach to money more and more strange.

But just what is money? Joe Dominguez, of the New Road Map Foundation, defines money as that which we trade for our "life energy." Our life energy is our own resource—our life. And, Dominguez further states, we usually trade our life energy for money through our employment (or self-employment). The acquisition of money has become so important that our means of acquiring it provides our most frequently used personal label—for example: I am a lawyer, plumber, car dealer, etc.

The purpose of money is to consume resources, as money generally buys things which are resources from the environment in one way or another. And since you have traded a piece of your life to get that money (through your employment), you are also consuming your own resource (your life energy) when you make and then spend money. By spending money, you are then creating a hole that seems to require you to "make" it back; that is what keeps the cycle going of trading your life energy for money through your employment.

In light of the above, it is extremely important—whatever you do to make money—that this money-making activity be:

(1) something that makes you unequivocably and totally happy, and

(2) something which is done with respect for our planet and all of its inhabitants.

You may be thinking, "Wow, that's a tall order. Is that really possible?" But my question is: Why should the activity at which you spend the bulk of your waking hours for the bulk of your able-bodied life be anything *less* than the above? After all, you are literally *spending your life* making your money.

Remember the beginning of this book? Life = Job. We could state this equation in another way: Making Money = Consuming Life.

Alan AtKisson, a former editor of *In Context* (a very fine periodical whose successor is now called *Yes! A Journal of Positive Futures*—see Appendix) goes a step further. Money, he says, "is the opposite of a gift. A gift is an expression of love and trust and community. Money, therefore, is an expression of our distrust and fear, and our basic separation from each other. It's not a 'measure of value.' It's a measure of our lack of love." Simply calling money a "medium of exchange" loses this point of money representing our lack of trust and our lack of connection with one another. This is why, for most of us, there has always been something that feels uncomfortable about money. Humans like—even thrive on—love, connection, and trust. If money is a measure of our lack of love, connection, and trust, it's no wonder that all of us have "money issues."

According to this philosophy, then, it makes sense to examine thoroughly all aspects of money—the activity you do to acquire it, and what you spend it on—to see if these things are in alignment with your values.

Author Ernest Callenbach has a helpful illustration about the effect of money in something he calls "The Green Triangle." The three points of the triangle are called MONEY, HEALTH, and ENVIRONMENT, and the triangle looks something like this:

Any time you do something beneficial for one of the points of the triangle, you will almost invariably do something beneficial for the other two. An example: eating less meat and dairy products. These foods are expensive, not good for human health, and damaging to the environment because of the intensive animal agriculture/factory farming practices. So, by eliminatingthem, you improve your health, save money, and help the environment. You can start at any point of the triangle and the other two points are quite likely to be affected in the same way.

Another example: riding a bicycle for transportation as much as possible. This will improve your health by the exercise and fresh air, help the environment by not running your car, and save you money by putting fewer miles on your car.

The converse of the above is also true. Any time you do something that *adversely* affects one of the points of the triangle, it is very likely that the other two points will be adversely affected also. I'm sure you can think of many examples in both directions.

The Green Triangle could be modified to become a square with a fourth point: (increasing) COMMUNITY. Actions which save money, improve one's health, and help the environment quite often increase the amount of *community* in one's life also. Such actions may involve sharing tools among neighbors, or sharing transportation with others. Other such actions may involve the need for greater coordination and communication among family members.

Community is an important ingredient that seems to be universally desired. It's interesting that the lifestyle choices which are expensive and taxing on the environment have also resulted in a decrease in community among people. Our society has definitely suffered from this decrease in community.

MORE HOMEWORK

OK, let's get practical. Here are suggestions which I have found to be invaluable.

- Examine the activity which earns you money. Is it truly *in alignment with your values*? Does it make you happy doing it? If you answer no to either question, putting in some heavy thought about changing the way you bring in money would be well worth your while. Remember: Making Money = Consuming Life.
- Keep in mind the previous chapter about calculating what it costs you to have your job. By all means, do this calculation, and then make adjustments accordingly.
- After doing your job costs calculations, you can then calculate how much money you really earn per hour of your life energy. Calculate all the time you spend working, perparing to go to work, and getting to and from work. Take that figure and divide it by your net income—*minus your job costs* (figuring all those costs with help from the previous chapter)—and you'll get your *true hourly wage*. You'll be surprised at how low this will be.
- Keep track of every cent you take in and spend—*every* cent both in and out. Carry around a little notebook with you to record this. At the end of each month, calculate the income and the outgo and note any difference in either direction. Then ask yourself, *with each expenditure*, "is this in alignment with my values?" In answering that question, be completely truthful with yourself. Plot your monthly calculations on a graph with separate lines for income and ex-

penses. Also, knowing your true hourly wage, you can calculate how many hours of your life energy an expenditure costs you. For example, if your true hourly wage is $5 per hour, you can ask yourself if a $20 shirt is truly worth 4 hours of your life energy. Over a period of the next few months you will naturally make adjustments as you honestly answer the "alignment" question. You will soon notice your expenses going down, and, just as importantly, your happiness and satisfaction about your lifestyle going up. (For this to be successful, I recommend that you do the above for at least one full year. Two or more years would be even better.)

• Keep evaluating in your mind as you go through these exercises exactly what you think your needs are that cost money. (Some needs—like love and fulfillment—do not cost money.)

Getting one's life in alignment with one's values is an ongoing path—it is not a final destination point at which one arrives. It's a *process*, the idea of which is to keep going further in the *direction* of alignment. This process never ends; but, it is a very joyous journey. Indeed, there are people who are happily and joyously living on incomes which many people would consider to be "poor" or "unfortunate." I am one of those people; and whether or not this kind of income is "poor" or "unfortunate" is all in the way one looks at it.

LOOKING AT PARTICULAR EXAMPLES

Allow me at this point to describe to you some of the

changes—ways I have reduced my expenses—this path of alignment has led me to. (Two of the biggest items which people are very concerned about—taxes and insurance—I am devoting entire chapters to. See Chapters VII and VIII.) As I take up these items, keep in mind "The Green Triangle" and the "alignment" principle.

Also, please keep in mind that these are my own personal choices. Each person will be different here. I'm briefly listing some of my choices to give you an example of one person's thinking and action regarding reducing expenses. There is no right or wrong here, just personal choices. Although no two people are alike in how they will make choices, I firmly believe that all people can reduce their expenses and be happier with lower expenses than with higher expenses. I will be discussing many of the very common major and minor categories of spending.

Housing is the first thing that comes to mind when considering expenses. Since World War II, Americans have lived in increasingly larger houses. Statistics show that the median size of a new house built in the US has doubled since the 1940s. Along with that, families are smaller, making the per capita square foot statistic even more of an increase.

Most people's biggest financial commitment is for living space—either rent or mortgage payment. In looking to lower our costs for shelter, my wife and I found that we could sell our house which had a large mortgage payment and buy a perfectly fine one in a less pricey part of town—and save bundles: the savings in our case amounted to about $500 a month—$6,000 per year that we wouldn't have to get through "jobbing." More importantly, we realized that it was possible to find a less expensive house which we would like more than the one we were in. In fact, all of this came to pass.

Others have found that renting a small apartment makes more sense. One couple I read about greatly reduced the amount of housing space they needed by greatly reducing their "stuff." They went from a 2,000+ square foot house full of things to a 650 square foot apartment; and they are quite happy. They went through a long and thorough process of what they are calling "unstuffing" to get to the point of being happier with 650 square feet than with more than 2,000 square feet. They now are quite open about their idea of "unstuffing." Greatly reducing one's cache of things can greatly reduce one's need for space, which can greatly reduce one's expenses, *which can greatly increase one's freedom to be who one wants to be!* In general, having less space usually encourages less accumulation of goods, which saves money, which can free up your life energy. Take a good look at how much living space you occupy, and how much you really need.

Food is a major expense for anyone. After all, we eat on a daily basis. And, the food we eat connects us to the entire web of life on Earth. It's important to think of food as something other than just "things" or "products" which we buy at a store called a supermarket. For many reasons, I eat only foods from the plant kingdom. This is a classic—perhaps *the* classic—"Green Triangle" example. The pure vegetarian foods are cheaper (in *true cost*, not necessarily in *price*), better for my health, and better for the environment. If you need convincing here, please read *Diet for a New America* and/or *May All Be Fed* by John Robbins. (See Appendix.) Those books will change your life. I cannot over-emphasize the importance of food, and what food we purchase. And, the Robins books are extremely well written and documented, making it very clear what effect the purchase of a certain food has on the web of life on the planet and on your personal health.

About the only thing I drink is water, for all the same "Green Triangle" reasons. I also avoid any food which is a "convenience" or over-packaged food or which is bought from a grocery freezer, again for the same "Green Triangle" reasons. So imagine the typical—and expensive—food items that, as a rule, I *happily* don't buy: beef, poultry, pork, fish, eggs, all dairy products, over-packaged, frozen, pre-cooked foods, soda, and all alcoholic beverages.

Mind you, this is not a deprivation campaign—I'm completely happy to be eating this way because it's best for my body, my planet, my pocketbook, and—especially—my values. How can I ignore such a combination of "best's"? (My food is also very tasty, and not boring, so there is no need to feel sorry for my taste buds.) I also don't recommend this type of food choosing merely to be a "cheapskate." The reasons I chose this diet were not initially about money. Saving money is merely an additional bonus.

The twentieth century post-industrial society has *drastically* changed what we consider to be normal foods, normal ways to produce these foods, and normal means of getting these foods from producer to consumer. Eating a better diet is cheaper for the consumer in more ways than one. Not only is brown rice, for example, cheaper than cheese, but the environmental costs to the planet and all life on it are far less. Unfortunately, we're typically so busy with our jobs that we can't or don't think about how we satisfy our hunger. Food merely becomes another product that we buy with our job-earned money. Nonetheless, this is such an urgently important topic, that it deserves everyone's complete, conscious attention.

One other thought: don't let the cheaper price of some foods fool you. Yes, many inferior foods have a lower *price*. But when you consider the medical and planetary costs (which we all bear), it's not cheaper at all. Again, there is a difference between *price* and *cost*.

Definitely think long and hard about your *car*. Along with food, the automobile is one of the major culprits in the problems of the world today. We all are contributing to that problem to the extent that we drive our cars. Our cars are also one of the biggest drains on our pocketbooks. If you happen to live in one of the few major cities in the US that has a real mass transit system, you might find it possible to do without a car completely. How fortunate! In such a city, taking public transportation and renting a car on those occasions when you wish to go out of town, will save you a great deal of money over owning your own car.

I don't live in a good public transportation city. So, I try to ask myself every time before I crank up the car, "is the positive represented by the purpose of this trip greater than the negatives represented by the running of the car for this trip?" Hopefully, I don't go unless I can answer the above question with a "yes."

More about cars: Absolutely put yourself out of the situation of having car *payments* (or payments of any kind except for housing). This includes payments for purchasing or leasing cars. Also, our family found that when we created a home-based life for ourselves, we could go from two cars to one; and that was a most happy move that definitely reduced our expenses. It's important for our society as a whole to ask the question, "need there be one car for every person aged 16 and older?" There are way too many cars in the world, and the driving factor (no pun intended) behind this is the Western competitive economic way of life.

I found that the daily *newspaper* just wasn't worth it when I held this item up to the triangle and alignment lights. A newspaper is about 65% advertisements. There's no denying that it is a vehicle for the destructive "growth" economics which I spoke about in Chapter 4. Of the remaining, non-commercial 35%, about one-fourth of that is sports, which I find myself less and less interested in, because sports are our society's way of legitmating "win-lose." And, I don't want to lend my energy to that cause any longer. That leaves only a little over one-fourth of the entire newspaper which even has a chance of interesting me. And, that 25% or so has dubious editorial choices in it. For example, one recent study indicated that, of the news content of a typical newspaper (only about 25% of an entire newspaper if you don't count sports), almost 40% of *that* in a recent year came from news releases and memos from large public relations firms. And, we all know where their interests lie.

Given all of the above, I decided that the newspaper just wasn't worth its cost of about $200 a year. I've found I can keep up with "what's going on in the world" and in my town without subscribing to the newspaper. (Actually, I frequently walk to my nearby public library branch, and sometimes look at the newspaper there.) Another thought: the wood pulp for a single issue of a Sunday *New York Times* requires the cutting of a small forest. And, 65% of those trees were cut for advertisements.

Over the last few decades, virtually all newspapers in this country have been bought out by about 15 large corporations, all of whom have similar "growth economics" interests. Obviously, they're interested not only in selling newspapers, but also in encouraging us to spend more money—our life energy—often for out of alignment things. This of course, makes it easier for newspapers to sell advertising, which allows newspaper people to better "make their living."

Opening ourselves to other ways of looking at the world gives us a healthier perspective that is more free from commercial interests, and it's likely to lower our expenses at the same time. This is another Green Triangle example.

Likewise, I found that *cable television* (and virtually all television) simply wasn't worth another roughly $200 a year to the cable company. I was too much into finding wonderful, inspirational books and doing my peace and justice endeavors. Besides, it seemed nonsensical to have three dozen choices of programs for every hour of every day, especially television with commercials which peddles materialism to irresponsible levels. The more I questioned TV regarding alignment, the less TV meant to me. On balance, not having a television at all would, in my mind, have more advantages than having one.

And consider *clothing*. I found that since I don't report to anybody, I have very little need to buy clothing. When I do see the need, I act according to ecological concerns and have come up with the following approach: First, I wear out an article of clothing completely. I don't care what the styles are, how un-new it looks, or how long I've had the article of clothing. If it functions and fits, I keep wearing it. At least for me, new-looking clothing or clothing in a variety of styles and colors is not important.

Second, when an article of clothing does wear out com-pletely, I look to replace it—if that is necessary—at a second-hand clothing store. I just love the idea of recirculating clothes among people. The clothes in the second-hand stores are often in very good condition, and they're very inexpensive. Most importantly, it's a good move for the environment not to buy newly-manufactured clothes.

Travel and entertainment are relatively low budget items in my household. I do very little going out to movies, restau-rants, and concerts. I do have a great need for social interaction; but that can be accomplished very satisfactorily, and inexpen-sively, with inviting friends over. I much prefer the more informal and personal kind of gathering at my home or other people's homes to going out to places of business.

I do some modest traveling, but major, transcontinental type excursions I am not doing. I have determined that this is a trade-off which is well worth it—the freedom and flexibility of the home-based, un-jobbed life is more important to me than traveling to whatever places that I would, admittedly, enjoy.

It's still possible to do major traveling within the "un-jobbing lifestyle." It would just need to be made a very high priority. My wife is much more interested in traveling than I am; and so, she budgets accordingly. Again, this is another example of the need to ask yourself what is in alignment with *your* values.

EACH OF US IS DIFFERENT

You may consider things like cable TV and the daily newspaper to be little things. And perhaps they are. The above are examples of expenses which I am happily doing without. But, they are my own personal examples. Different people will make different choices. That is why I haven't gone into great amounts of detail about how I have reduced my expenses personally. There are an abundance of books and periodicals on frugality, and ways to lower your expenses. Some of these resources are cited in the Appendix. Again, a major point here is that un-jobbing involves lowering expenses not to be some sort of "cheapskate," but to create for yourself a life of freedom and a life geared increasingly toward your joys and your heart-felt values, rather than a life oriented toward chasing money to meet ever increasing expenses.

You will notice when you do the recommended exercises in this chapter that there are numerous little expenses in your life which you may have hardly thought about. And to be sure, these little expenses that everyone has do add up. Usually, people don't think about these little expenses, because they are too busy doing their jobs. Yet, it is precisely the thinking about these things, and the making of adjustments accordingly, which can make for increased happiness, freedom, and satisfaction in one's life.

WHAT ABOUT BEING GOOD TO OURSELVES?

Often, we spend money as a "treat" to ourselves because we've been working hard at our jobs. (Translated: we've been putting up with spending our lives doing an activity which is not truly where our hearts want us to be. And, deep down, we know that that is a great deal to put up with.) So, to be "good to ourselves," we spend some money on something that is basically frivilous and out of alignment. Of course, that only adds to the pressure of "needing" to earn still more money from our jobs.

And, again, there is nothing wrong with spending money, *if* you are doing it with a highly aware consciousness that what you are spending the money on feels good to you and is in alignment with your values after thoroughly examining all aspects of the expenditure. As I said earlier, this is not meant to put you on a deprivation campaign, and it's not an issue of personal sacrifice. This is a matter of values and relationship. What is our relationship to Earth and its inhabitants, and how do we value it? And, how do we value our own lives and our time that we have to live our lives?

Acting on an honest answer to those questions, we begin to take great *joy* in spending less. For me, spending less *is* being good to myself. There is no sense of sacrifice or deprivation at all when this is done with the proper thought and understanding behind it. I only recommend that you reduce your expenses with total joy. The world may be better off with your being happy about spending a lot, rather than being miserable and feeling deprived about spending little.

Going through life feeling deprived will defeat the purpose

of the principles I am espousing in this book. If you find yourself feeling that way, keep asking yourself the alignment question, and listen to your heart. By doing that, there should be no room for deprivation.

The bottom line for me is that I've been able to "make ends meet" with what is for modern western society relatively little income because I've greatly reduced my expenses. And, most importantly, I'm very *satisfied* doing things this way. Spending less money has purpose other than just being miserly.

We've discussed some common categories of spending including some so-called "little" things; so, let's go on to those two big topics: taxes and insurance. For most people, those definitely represent large items in the expense column.

CHAPTER 7

(UNLIKE DEATH)
TAXES ARE NOT CERTAIN

I would be hard-pressed to come up with a word that dredges up more *nervousness* and more downright *fear* than the word "taxes." Only the name "IRS" creates the same mix of emotions. Like "making a living" and the Industrial Revolution, income taxes—at least to the extent that they are a major part of our lives now—are only an historically very recent phenomenon.

As was mentioned earlier, the history of the income tax in the modern western industrial world largely parallels the history of warfare—hot and cold. And—not news to anyone—warfare in recent times has become *very* expensive. Follow the history of income taxes and you will quickly see that, as our nation went to war, our income taxes went up. And, that means our personal expenses, and the pressure to make more money, also went up. This is the reason why I have devoted an entire chapter to taxes. Taxes are inextricably connected to "making a living" (see below); and therefore an un-jobber needs to have a conscious understanding of this issue.

A BRIEF TAX HISTORY

At first, income taxes were collected in person by tax collectors once a year. The problem was that many people, whose forté was not advance planning, simply had to say to the tax collector, "I don't have the money." This problem was fixed, though, by the ingenious plan of withholding taxes from paychecks. Under this plan, employers took money each pay period from the employees to send to the government before the employees even saw the money. As you might imagine, this was met with *considerable* dislike, especially as taxation was extended to those at lower and lower income levels. But people gradually got used to the tax and the withholding of money from paychecks.

Ironically, the withholding became more palatable to the public when, later, this withholding began to *increase* resulting in—for most people—more tax withheld than what the employee would end up owing at the end of the year. Thus, even though greater amounts of money were being taken from the employee's paycheck, the IRS began to be, in the minds of many people, a *refunder* of money instead of a *collector* of money. What an ingenious way to turn around the psychology of siphoning money out of people's paychecks: take out even more, so that filling out tax return forms becomes a way for the people to get a check *from* the government. Of course, anyone who gets a refund from the IRS has merely loaned the government money at 0% interest. That's a poor form of a savings account.

In fact, this whole arrangement is misleading and confusing to people in many ways; a person earning a salary of, say,

$2,000 a month seems to think of their salary as something closer to $1,200. Somehow, in what we've fooled ourselves into thinking is a completely separate action, a magical gift from Uncle Sam is doled out every April.

WHY THIS IS IMPORTANT FOR UN-JOBBERS

The point of all this is that, in just a few generations, the tax bite has increased as rapidly as the cultural "need" for making more and more money. This has become a kind of "one-two punch" on the citizen of the modern society creating tremendous pressure to earn increasing amounts of money. And, to earn more money, it is necessary to sell more things or services.

In fact, high consumption and high taxation very much go hand in hand, although most people don't see the connection. By consuming less, not only would we have smaller tax bills, but also society as a whole would see less need for the tax revenues. Thus, while war-making established the income tax, the need for tax revenues is fueled by our consumeristic way of life. The more we spiral up consumeristic economics, the more the gap between the rich and the poor widens, and the more the gap between the rich and the poor widens, the more there is a need for tax-supported government social programs to help the "have-nots." In addition, the more consumeristic a society is, the more that society seems to see the need for heavy military spending to "defend it's way of life." Now we're back to how income taxes started in the first place. It's no coincidence whatsoever that the United States is both the most materialistic society on Earth and the greatest military power.

PAYING TAXES IS SPENDING MONEY (LIFE ENERGY)

So, just what does the federal government do with our tax money? Since our taxpaying is just as much a category of personal spending as, say, our food purchasing, it's important to examine our taxpaying from the aligning with values point of view. Currently, Americans send roughly about $1 trillion per year to the federal government in income taxes. What are we getting for that money?

When one gathers it all together, military spending comes to about 50% of the income tax-derived expenditures—that is, those expenditures carried out with money from income taxes, not money from other sources like separately funded programs such as social security and medicare/medicaid.

Furthermore, when I started looking into the other (non-military) income tax-derived expenditures of the US government and applied them to my "alignment" question, I became uncomfortable with much of that spending, too. I realized that institutions like the Department of Agriculture were very much oriented toward helping economic "growth" of (mainly big-time) farmers and multinational agribusiness and basically ignoring the human health and environmental consequences of its policies and funding actions. I realized that the government encourages our country's addiction to the automobile, to tobacco, and to our generally toxic, throw-away way of life. It does this with things like "price supports," legislation, "pork barrel" projects, grants, and loans which may or may not be paid back.

The US government, with its Gross Domestic Product

mentality, really doesn't care what things people are buying and selling, as long as we are doing plenty of both. When that seems to be happening, it is declared that we are in "good economic times." Never mind that much of this activity involves waste and environmental and human devastation, not to mention unfulfilled lives. On top of all this, we've all heard about how relatively good programs in the federal government with really good intentions are inefficiently, or even corruptly, run. In short, as the line from *Mary Poppins* goes, "we have a ghastly mess."

AND WE'RE ALL PAYING FOR IT WITH OUR LIFE ENERGIES AND, FOR THE MOST PART, WE'RE DOING THIS UNCONSCIOUSLY!

In fact, the only way human beings can tolerate this kind of a mess is that we somehow convince ourselves to consider the money taken from our paychecks which pays for this ghastly mess as not ours in the first place.

But it is the citizens' money. And, unfortunately, the more we spiral up the destructive cycle of economic "growth" by focusing on ever increasing our income earning, the more we rely on that great bureaucratic institution in Washington to "make our lives better." This, in turn, fuels the government with more of our tax money, encouraging even more expenditures by the government, thereby increasing our incredible national debt.

I've saved the most intriguing bit of information for last. According to people who took the time and trouble to research this, it turns out that the 16th Amendment, which supposedly makes the income tax "legal," was not even properly ratified! Many states were counted as having ratified the amendment when one or both of their legislative houses actually voted against it. Then, it seems that then-US Secretary of State, Philander Knox, simply "declared" the 16th Amendment ratified. Remember, this was 1913, before the days of television and other instant forms of communication and verification. (For more information, see *The Law That Never Was*, in the Appendix.)

BRINGING CONSCIOUSNESS BACK INTO OUR TAXPAYING

I mention all of this because I think people should do everything in their lives in a totally aware and conscious way. Since World War II, the income tax situation has been a classic case of "pulling the wool over our eyes." We've cooperated with it virtually unconsciously and with a lot of fear because we feel intimidated by the IRS.

After seeing that, and noting all of the out-of-alignment (for me) expenditures that the federal government makes, I decided that this was another major reason to get out of the job-dominated life. With a home-based life centered around truly living and serving, and not centered around increasing my money intake, I am also not sending my money to the US government. I believe that there are simpler, more joyous, more truly democratic (people empowering), and more effective ways of creating our common good than by channeling our money through Washington. These ways involve local community self-reliance—not individual isolationism—but small-scale, human-scale ways of taking care of one another. There are avenues in this realm which our society has barely even begun to explore or think about.

I now consider myself a "peace taxpayer." That means I believe in the necessity of people banding together and pooling resources in order to take care of our common good. This does involve taxation to some extent, but "peace taxpaying" means that I wish to make my tax spending pay for *only* life-enhancing, peaceful, environmentally non-toxic things, which are in alignment with my values. I believe that I have the right to live according to my conscience, and that I have the right to freely exercise my conscienciously held beliefs as long as that exercise harms no one else. How could I, as a peace activist, work for peace, and pray for peace, and then pay for war, environmental destruction, and corruption? If I sent dollars to the US government, about half of those dollars would go to pay for past, present, and future wars. It would be the same as my spending half of the money that I do for food, as a vegetarian, on meat. It makes no sense.

I avoid paying federal income taxes in ways that, even according to the IRS, are legal. But, avoidance has a negative connotation to it, and I always want to be for something rather than against something; so, let me put this in a *positive* way. I'm getting closer and closer to the point where everything I do spend money on—including the tax paying I do—is in alignment with my values.

I don't earn a taxable income, but make no mistake, I'm still very much a taxpayer. There are many local, state, utility, and even some federal taxes that I pay in which I at least see some basic good. As well, I take great joy in making modest monetary contributions directly to the causes I wish to support. There is some good that is done with our federal income tax money. But it's such an incredibly small percentage of the total that it makes no sense to me to send money to the federal government and feel good about maybe a scant few cents out of every dollar I would pay. How many other purchases do we make in which 50% or less of the product purchased makes us feel good? If that is something that makes no sense, why do we put up with this situation regarding income taxes? Much of this book is dealing with the theme of getting one's expenses in alignment with one's values. There is no need to have taxpaying off limits from this principle. It, too, can be included in one's alignment evaluations.

You may have very different views about federal income taxes. Your answers to the alignment question may be very different from mine. The main point with this chapter is to be very aware of the whole situation—where the money comes from, where it goes, and how consistent that is with one's values. Then, when that understanding is present, one can work on being more in control of this category of personal spending (life energy).

The good thing for me is that I have solved this personal dilemma because my life outside of "making a living" happens to put me "legally" in a nontaxable income bracket. And I really like all the ramifications of that.

CHAPTER 8

THE GAMBLE OF INSURANCE

A major expense for most people in this society is insurance—your car, your house, your body, your life. Insurance has been around for quite some time, but it's only been in recent decades that it has really taken off as an industry. Why? We're so hooked on the need to make lots of money through our "making a living" that an entire industry has spawned "ensuring" that, in the case we can no longer make that money, we can continue in the same (wasteful) lifestyle. This entire industry is itself yet another way for a large and growing number of people to "make their living."

And, like taxes, insurance plays on the great emotion *fear*. "What if I catch a disease or I somehow can't make this salary, and I can't afford the house payment, and the car payment, and to buy this or that...?" What if, what if, what if. Those two little words have earned the insurance industry more money than the inventors of this industry (dare I say "scheme"?) probably ever dreamed possible.

The whole reason that insurance seems to have become a "necessity" is that we have created this economic way of life of the vicious circle of making products and getting products, instead of the economy based on giving and getting service. If our economic way of life were based on the latter idea, the insurance industry would have no ground on which to stand.

WHAT INSURANCE REALLY IS

I once heard a news story about the gambling casino industry. This news story very frankly stated the major principle behind how this industry is "successful": every once in a great while give very small numbers of people a payoff—just enough so that very large numbers of people constantly keep paying in money. When I reflected on that, it suddenly dawned on me that that is exactly how the insurance industry "succeeds," only with the insurance industry, the people who get a "payoff" have in many cases, had something catastrophic (or nearly catastrophic) happen to them.

In short, taking out an insurance policy is a bet, a gamble. Even the insurance industry admits this. The insurance industry is betting that you are not going to make a claim, and that they can merrily continue to collect money, called "premiums," from you. At the very least, the insurance industry is betting that they will be making a profit on you over the course of your lifetime; that is, if you do receive any "benefits," those benefits will be more than offset by your payments to the company over the course of your lifetime. This can't be any surprise. After all, that's the basic premise of all businesses—pay out less money than you take in. Yet, somehow, the industry has convinced the policy-holder to bet that the money s/he pays in will come back in benefits. (Otherwise, why take up this deal?) This brings up three points: (1) Can peace of mind actually be bought? (2) Why would anyone want to bet that their house will burn down or that they will be in critical, catastrophic health; and (3) even if you don't like the second question, *GUESS WHO IS WINNING THE BET?!*

Even if you don't see insurance as a gamble, it is crystal clear that the insurance business is a for profit, big industry. Some insurance companies may officially be cooperatives or non-profit corporations. But, this industry does not risk losing money. Making a profit from policyholders is why the industry exists. This is true for any kind of policy from any kind of insurance comapny. This industry does not take on a single policy with any individual unless it thinks that, in all probability, the balance of payments will be in *its* favor. Much more often than not, they're right. And, that's why this industry has been such a "successful" avenue for "making a living." If an insurance company believes that the balance of payments will not be in its favor, it usually denies selling a policy in such a case.

BUT WHAT ABOUT...?

When I tell people that I don't have a job with fringe benefits, many people get this worried, sympathetic look on their faces—"What about health insurance?"

As we all know, the amount of money we've been paying for medical services in the United States is totally beyond reason. Some of that is definitely due to a health care system based on the insurance industry, in which profit is part of the picture of our taking care of our health. But some of it is due to a similar factor that was discussed in the previous chapter: people don't want to take responsibility for their own health.

The healthcare crisis is not really about how we are going to pay the bills. The crisis is the lifestyle we follow, and the attitudes we cling to, which have created such high bills. Life-threatening diseases, from heart disease to various cancers, are running rampant in our affluent Western society. These are the so-called "diseases of civilization." They might even be called Industrial Revolution/Jobbing diseases. Most of us want medical science to come up with a drug or a surgical procedure or one of those incredibly expensive machines for (hopefully early) detection and treatment of a disease. All of these avenues are very expensive, and are geared to fixing things that are wrong, rather than preventing disease. The insurance, medical, and pharmaceutical industries have merely seized upon the opportunity to increase their capacity to "make their livings."

So, what's going on? Because of our "way of life" (of earn and earn, spend and spend, and the ramifications thereof), our health is suffering; rather than taking responsibility for ourselves and changing our lifestyles, we'd prefer *paying someone else to "fix" us.* (This, of course, just means that we have to earn still more money, which in all likelihood will take us further down the road which created this "need" in the first place.)

Let's face it: the way to good health is no secret. It is simple, clear, and, quite happily, inexpensive: (1) ingest only those substances which are healthful for the human body—whole grains, vegetables (including legumes), and fruits; do this in good variety and go easy on fat, especially tropical oils and hydrogenated fat; (2) get plenty of fresh air, time outside, and exercise; (3) don't induce stress on yourself by over-"working" or fearful worry; and (4) spend your life loving yourself and all those around you while doing what makes you happy.

I think that deep in our hearts we all know the above to be true; all we need to do is follow the above principles. But, instead, many of us live a life denying these principles and depending on a system of paying someone else to attempt to give us good health—to, in effect, "right our wrongs."

Of course, none of us will go through our entire life without some disease or injury. But, if one follows the above principles, the health problems that will happen are much more likely to be smaller and less expensive to deal with than the health problems that would occur not following the above principles.

Eating a plant-based diet, exercising, and being a loving, non-workaholic person is not only a very inexpensive way to live, it also is a very blessed way to live. Such a person is truly blessed—with good health and much happiness. Furthermore, I see it as no more a gamble to be living that type of life than living the typical "making a living" life and paying for health insurance.

To be sure, there are those among us who live with a disease which requires some medical attention. Society needs to help our fellow humans in such a situation, but not in the way our current system does it. As far as I am concerned, if I should someday get cancer, I don't think I would want the expensive treatments of western, allopathic medicine, anyway. I don't think I would want my body to be toxically invaded with radiation or chemotherapy. There are other, definitely less expensive, and probably more satisfying and joyful ways of dealing with disease. More than likely these ways would cost less than a lifetime of monthly payments to an insurance policy (and the deductibles and co-payments).

If you feel you must have something in the way of health insurance, then check into a catastrophic policy which covers only major expenses, usually with a very high deductible, up to $5,000 for example. (There is a way to do this with a "socially responsible" company, which has a wide-ranging acceptance of different kinds of medical approaches and treatments, through Co-op America. See Appendix.) That way, you are at least claiming responsibility for all but major, catastrophic health problems that may come up. Such a high deductible, catastrophic policy is relatively inexpensive, although it would still be a considerable ongoing monthly expense.

Another option is to pay insurance premiums to yourself. This could be an account that you put your "premiums" into and leave untouched except for health care expenses. When you have a health care expense, you draw the money out. It not, you leave it alone. If you are truly taking care of yourself, chances are the years will go by, and you will be accumulating the money instead of an insurance company.

My family and I are taking a greater "risk," some would say, by not having even the $5,000 deductible type of health insurance. When we have a health care expense, we simply pay for it. These expenses are very infrequent and quite small compared to an ongoing health insurance policy. But the bottom line for me is that I have grown to feel perfectly comfortable, safe, and happy without it. This decision feels good.

No decision about health insurance is completely without risk. Merely being an alive human on Earth entails risk. Weighing all the paramaters about health insurance is a personal decision which one person cannot make for another. Putting in some serious thought about how you are *creating, proactively,* your own health is strongly advised. There are many, many strategies which would create a strong hedge against the risk of being an alive person on Earth.

WHAT ABOUT THE HOUSE AND THE CAR?

Definitely examine what you have in the way of house and car insurance and ask yourself if you really need your policies. In many states car insurance is forced upon people in order to have license plates on the car. If you feel you must have car insurance, have the smallest policy you can have with the highest deductibles you are comfortable with. Of course, if you can live without a car, you won't need car insurance.

With your house, the same suggestions apply: if you feel you must have it (perhaps your mortgage company requires it) then get the smallest policy possible with the highest deductibles you are comfortable with. If you achieve the fortunate position of owning a house outright, you have the golden opportunity to examine this issue without pressure from the mortgage lender. The main thing to keep in mind is that the insurance company would not be interested in selling you a bigger policy if it weren't going to make a bigger profit from you by such a sale. By selling you extra insurance they know that, from their point of view, it's a very good bet indeed.

THE GAMBLE OF INSURANCE

In summary, insurance in general should be thought of as an *option*, a choice you can make if you wish, given all the particulars of your situation. This industry has been very successful, however, in getting society to see its "products" as "needs." Viewing insurance, as the expensive, generally losing gamble that it is, as a need, shows me just how distorted our present-day cultural-line about this issue has become.

Insurance is not a need. It's a possible option that is, much more often than not, a losing bet for the policy holder. The insurance industry tries to get across the opposite point of view by using such euphemistic expressions as "coverage" and "protection" and "peace of mind" when describing what they sell. The truth is that the only things you are doing *for certain* when you buy insurance are (1) helping pay for other people's salaries, and in some cases very large salaries; and (2) putting pressure on your own need for earning income in order to cover the costs. In the case of (1), we hear of large, even "non-profit," insurance companies with executives who make salaries in the six figures. In the case of (2), the pressure on income earning to cover the costs of insurance in contemporary western society has become very great. This is especially true in the United States with regard to health insurance. Indeed, insurance in general is another case of something getting way out of hand.

The more we can create a society of local self reliant communities with people taking care of one another—getting and giving service—the less there will be a perceived need for massive institutionalized "solutions" like insurance. The topic of insurance is very important for un-jobbers not only because it is a potentially very large expense, but also because of the psychology and philosophy contained therein.

CHAPTER 9

YOUR CONSCIOUS PLAN FOR LIBERATION

One of my favorite slogans in the peace movement through the years has been: "question authority." Now, however, that idea means much more to me than it once did. I used to think it merely meant that when the government (or some other "authority") said something, I didn't automatically believe it. But, "question authority" has now taken on a broader meaning to me. When any person, institution, bureaucratic entity, or society says (or *seems* to say) that I "have" to do something, I now don't automatically and unconsciously *comply*. The words "you've got to" are slowly, but surely, being erased from my thinking. If what I'm being "required" to do makes sense to me and is in line with what I feel is the truth, fine. But if not, I can freely choose to do something different as long as I harm no one else. To do this is an inalienable right as a human being. This is the key to truly conscious living.

Perhaps we could change this slogan to "question convention." Conventions to question? Things like handing over money to the government for programs which cause nasty environmental and human devastation; things like handing over money to insurance companies under a false sense of security that it will make us safe and healthy; things like allowing a school system geared toward competitive "growth" economics to teach and practically rear our children, when many of us would rather have our children learn and grow up in other, more cooperative ways—for example by allowing them to learn in a home-based self-directed way (something my wife and I are doing with our son); and things like spending the bulk of our waking hours of our adult lives "making a living" in a job which is perhaps giving us only a mild sense of satisfaction and fulfillment.

Perhaps the biggest notion I am questioning is the old adage that we must "take the bad with the good." Must we? Can we not do and participate in only good—at least as far as the vast majority of our time, energy, and resources are concerned? At the very least, it seems that how we spend the bulk of our waking hours of our adult lives could be on the whole a satisfactory, joyous, and ecologically-sustainable activity. To me, that doesn't seem too much to ask.

The main point of the philosophy of un-jobbing is— whatever you do—do what you do because you truly want to, because it brings you and others great joy and love, because you *consciously*—with total awareness of all factors—have *freely* chosen to do it. Again, we should consider this way of choosing to be our inalienable right as a creature of the Universe.

Doing things because you feel like you're in a trap or a box formed by society, in which you must exist, follow orders, make your money, and endure your time during this life is very unfortunate. That's playing the role of the victim, rather than playing the role of the chooser and the creator of your reality.

The victim role is the mentality of the "no-fault" life (like "no-fault" insurance). I prefer assuming total responsibility for my life (with help, of course, from my own support community which everyone should have); and by doing this, I can experience much greater joy, and, as a consequence, I can spill that joy out to others.

NO ONE IS STUCK

It's amazing how, when one makes the choice to be his or her own choreographer, things go very well—not necessarily as one might think or predict—but very well nonetheless. When my wife and I were contemplating "leaping off the cliff" and leaving our guaranteed salaried jobs, we were certainly somewhat afraid. But, as we worked through things, and talked with friends, we had a great revelation: we have—everybody has—*options*. No one is "stuck" with anything. There are *always* options.

In looking at options, we asked ourselves, "How *will* we meet our expenses?" The first thing we realized was how simple and inexpensive basic human needs are—(1) enough food to satisfy your hunger, (2) enough clothes to keep you warm, (3) shelter to protect you from the elements in which there is a reasonable temperature, and (4) love. These are basically very simple and, for the most part, very inexpensive. And notice that the word "jobs" does not appear on the above list of true needs. We can let ourselves and our inner voices tell us what we need, instead of being fed "needs" through such societal avenues as TV and radio commercials and print advertisements.

I am struck by a survey which showed that about 5% of those making $15,000 a year or less said that they had achieved the "American Dream." At the greater than $50,000 a year level, only 6% said that they had achieved the "American Dream." From these statistics and other research done on this issue, it's clear that money has little to do with happiness or fulfillment. That finding has been proven over and over again.

The story I related earlier about our moving to a less expensive house is a good example of the worth of opening ourselves up to other options. Until we sold our previous house, though, we had to get comfortable with some temporary "deficit spending." If you have some modest reserves, as we did, this is a reasonable decision in making a transition in your life—as long as you know the deficit period is finite, and that soon you will be able to spend less than you take in.

In my own family's case, opening ourselves to options has really brought miracles into our lives. By seeing "you've got to" as an option which we are free to choose or not, our eyes have opened to other options. And the more we have opened our eyes to options, the more free we have become. It's liberating, and it's joyous.

During Joe Dominguez's seminars about people's relationship with money, there were times when people in the audience almost exploded with the realization that they could quit their jobs immediately and be financially independent for the rest of their lives. They could do this because, with lower expenses achieved by using the "alignment" principle, the interest on their savings would support them fully! But some people don't realize the potential inherent in their current resources, because they are too busy "making a living" until the age of 65 to notice! Perhaps right now, you are sitting on your own gold mine, but don't even realize it! Take a hard look at what your needs really are and what wealth you already have. The former may be much less than you think, and the latter may be much more than you think!

Many people who have followed the New Road Map Foundation's program have actually taken the time (usually several years) and achieved *financial independence.* They've done this by reducing their expenses, and then putting away money in investments, the interest from which equals what they need to live on. Most of the people who have achieved this, have done it within about 10 years. The main catch with this is that it does take a fairly large income in order to be able to sock away enough money to retire well before "retirement age." But, just imagine. People in this situation actually have *no need to make money. Everything* they do can consist of activities which they love to do and which are in complete alignment with their values. Their lives can be ones of service without charging anything for what they do. Just imagine it.

In my own case, I was not in a position, nor did it seem I could put myself in a position, of making enough money for some years to have the investments to achieve financial independence. It also seemed that even if I could get such a job, it most likely wouldn't be in alignment with my values (this wouldn't necessarily be the case with everybody); and, I would have to put up with that for a number of years. Besides, as I recounted in Chapter 2, I didn't do very well in this department. Therefore, it seemed best in my situation to *act*, in effect, as if I had achieved this financial independence anyway.

YOUR CONSCIOUS PLAN FOR LIBERATION

I now think of my life as one of service and one in which my activities are in alignment with my values. This is purely a psychological attitude, but it's possible to dis-attach "work" from the money paid for that work. I do need to earn some money; but, as I've stated throughout this book, the amount of that needed income has been brought down to a low level. And, the activities which I do to earn the money are activities which I most want to do in the world anyway. As well, we have found some aspects of financial independence within our grasp, even without actually having it.

For example, my wife, who had worked for about fifteen years as a University professor, left that situation to do what she consciously wanted to do—return her gifts to the community in her own way. (She is using music as a catalyst for healing, something the academic institution discouraged.) Many thought she was crazy, but things have worked out well. Because of her years as a faculty member, she looked into the option of receiving her retirement annuity. While most of the academic world works until around the age of 65, we found that she could start getting a monthly annuity payment more than twenty years before turning 65. She will receive this monthly payment for the rest of her life. Happily, it almost exactly equals our current mortgage payment. Bingo!

Of course, you may be thinking, "Well, that was a stroke of luck for him. I don't have a spouse with a pension." That's okay. We are not *dependent* on that pension at all; that pension merely frees us up even more than if we didn't have it. We would be managing fine without it. Money can come from many sources; and—except for ethical considerations—it's not important what the sources are. What's important is that the way you are occupying your time fits your heart. When that happens, and especially if you have a good handle on your true needs as well, then I believe that Life (with a capital "L") will support you in one way or another. Follow your heart and be open and flexible about where money can come from. Your support doesn't have to be in the form of a paycheck. And, the point of mentioning my wife's pension is that we had, and many people also have, monetary wealth that just needed to be uncovered. Look around, and see what you find.

HOW DO UN-JOBBERS EARN WHAT INCOME THEY NEED?

Most of us will need to do something to bring in a little cash if we give up our salaried employment. Charles Long in *How to Survive Without a Salary* (see Appendix) refers to this as "casual income." That term brings such a wonderful, relaxed connotation to the necessity to earn some amount of money. This is just the opposite of all the baggage carried in the words "career" and "job" and "occupation." This baggage, of course, is something we have put upon ourselves; and we are perfectly free to remove it as well.

So, how will you earn your "casual income"? I'm a firm believer that we all have our own unique gifts and talents. It is up to each individual, of course, to discover what they are. With expenses naturally and happily reduced, though, you can have much less pressure on yourself about the *amount* of money you need to bring in.

YOUR CONSCIOUS PLAN FOR LIBERATION

Here are some examples of how some people who have un-jobbed—given up a major, full-time, "career" job—are earning money, their casual income:

• A single woman who quit her job with a stock brokerage after 10 years, has done the following: she works in a flower shop one or two days a week (she loves flowers, but that amount of time is sufficient for her to satisfy this love); and she moved out of her large, expensive house and rents it while living herself in a small, inexpensive apartment. She managed to pay off her house; and that means that the rent from this rather pricey home supplies her with most of the income she needs.

• A co-habitating man derives some income from a family farm. He lives on this farm and oversees the work done by a tenant farmer. The rest of of his income comes from distributing a monthly alternative newspaper and freelance editorial work. The editorial work is his true love; and, he's finding ways to bring in income from this kind of work.

• A married couple with 2 children live out in the country. She does part-time nursing. He does an occasional carpentry job. They all do as much growing of their own food as they can. The children are homeschoolers. They've even been able to take fascinating trips to Central America and China with creative fund-raising. The husband has cut down on the self-employment work he does, because it works out better in the total financial picture!

• Another married couple with 2 children live in a very

inexpensive "handyman's special." It works: he's a handyman, and he makes enough income from word-of-mouth odd jobs to keep the family of four afloat. Their housing expense is very little.

• A single woman who quit a high-powered, high income computer consulting job, now does the same work but on a self-employed, freelance basis. Since her income needs are relatively low, she does it only as much as she wishes; and when she does do it, she earns well.

• A widower without a pension (except for social security) makes enough income to support himself by teaching classes in English as a second language. He really enjoys this teaching; and he lives very cheaply in a small apartment.

• An accountant who shares a house with a roommate quit her job and now has her own bookkeeping service at which she works about 2 days a week. She also does some freelance writing that brings in a little money. She has plenty of free time to do community volunteer work that she wants to do.

• One of the new things I have done to earn income is to present the ideas in this book in Voluntary Simplicity workshops. The demand is great; and I'm doing what I love. Your area might have a need for this, too. I also use my musical gifts to earn money.

Of course, any freelance, self-employed activity could turn into the major full-time job that we're all trying to get away from. Remember the principles: freedom with time, flexibility, an activity in alignment with values, financial needs at a low level, thinking in terms of *casual income*, not major career-building.

If you are in a job right now which you would like to leave, there may very well be *aspects* of it that you truly enjoy. Think about how those aspects you enjoy could be done on your own to earn income. For example, a man I met loved computers, but greatly disliked what his job was doing even though it involved computers. So, he quit his job and began carving out work with computers on his own that he would be happy about.

The main thing is, that whatever you do for money, make it something that is joyful for you and whose primary purpose is to spread love. If it is something that you would want to be doing *regardless of the money*, because it brings you great joy, then I believe you will have the money you need to live just fine. "Do what you love, the money will follow" really is true, if you faithfully believe in it.

If when doing something you feel loving and happy, then that's the best indication that you are doing the right thing in the right amount. (Notice the two components of the previous sentence: right thing *and* right amount. We all need space in our lives just to *be*, rather than constantly *doing*. (After all, we are called human *beings*, aren't we?) But, if you start pressuring yourself, and earning money becomes the primary purpose of whatever activity you do, then it will definitely lose the effect of giving you fulfillment. The primary purpose needs to be centered on joy and love—the money will follow.

UN-JOBBING

A LIFESTYLE THAT INCLUDES TIME

One of the plagues of our society is our chronic national busy-ness (just like the word "business"). How many people in this society would "love" to do something if they "only had the time"? Why aren't people doing things they "would love to do"? Certainly, the world would be a better place if more people were able to "somehow find the time" to do the things which they truly feel drawn to do.

Somehow, our lifestyle designed around working 40 or more hours a week at something which may very well *not* be what a person would love to do is getting in the way. In his novel, *Ecotopia*, Ernest Callenbach describes a fictional society in which the "work week" is 20 hours. Ecotopia also seemed to be a society in which people could more easily follow their hearts. Unemployment was unheard of, and no one seemed to lack for "security" in any way—*and* people had time on their hands to do and to be in ways in which they were drawn. He says in the book, "the distinction between work and non-work seems to be eroding away in Ecotopia, along with our [the American] whole concept of jobs as something separate from 'real life.' Ecotopians, incredibly enough, enjoy their work." I think it's amazing to think that it's incredible that a society of people would enjoy their work! The fact that that is a foreign notion to contemporary westerners is appalling.

Of course, Ecotopia is a fictional place. But, there is no reason that here in the "real world" we can't at least, for now, individually claim our right to spend our life energies in ways which make our hearts ring true. If greater numbers of individuals followed this philosophy, then eventually we would see more of a societal movement toward this. Part of many people's hesitancy with making life changing moves, is that so few other people are doing it. Indeed, more courage is necessary to do something that fewer people are doing than to do something that large masses of people are doing. Nonetheless, if the courage can be mustered, happiness and fulfillment will surely follow.

For courage to be different, I highly recommend the classic books by Helen and Scott Nearing called *Living the Good Life*, *Continuing the Good Life*, and *Loving and Leaving the Good Life*. The Nearings were the quintessential homesteaders, but, it won't matter if you're not interested in going "back to the land." These books are very inspiring. They get across the point of having meaning and consciousness in your life in a very wonderful way. And, the Nearings did this for decades in the United States. They always had an income-producing activity, and they always had plenty of free time for reading, music, receiving visitors, and traveling to lecture about "the good life." Their idea was that "bread work," which included what they did for casual income and the work necessary to build and maintain their home and garden, should occupy no more than half the day. The rest of the time should be spent on whatever pursuits resonate with one's heart. See Appendix.

As I choose more options away from "the rat race," I've gotten much closer to the amazing world that passes most people by. Now that I have time to sit and think on my front porch or go to the park with my son or do all kinds of things during "business hours" when most people are "at work," I've noticed a sense of calm and peace in the world that I never knew before.

Listening to the birds on a Monday morning, for example,

UN-JOBBING

I am struck by the fact that they are merely doing what makes them happy. They're just freely being birds. On that same Monday morning, millions and millions of human beings are filing into factories and office buildings. It strikes me that most of these people are not freely being what free and natural human beings ought to be. While the birds know how to be free and natural birds, a great many human beings have shut out the options of freely and naturally pursuing humanly joyful activities. The great shame is that so many people hardly even know what they are missing.

If you've read this far, you have opened yourself up to the possibility of exploring your options—and there are several besides immediately walking away from your job. You don't necessarily have to "leap off a cliff." Un-jobbing for you, at first, may mean looking for a clearer understanding of what your present job is; then, perhaps it can be a much less dominating, pre-occupying factor in your life. You may start doing things in your job for love—returning your gifts—rather than for "getting ahead." You can begin to reduce the costs (financial and otherwise) of having your job. You may decide that your job *is* what you would most want to be doing after you've applied the principles espoused in this book. (In that case, your salary will seem much larger, because you will be spending much less.) Or you may come up with a plan for leaving your job at some future time for a home-based, un-jobbed life and doing "your own thing."

Since I have left the jobbing world, I have realized things which I literally couldn't see before that departure. One of the most important of these realizations is that the physical environment that I find myself in has a major impact on me. I find tremendous peace and joy in being in my home which is very comfortable for me, which allows me to exist in lots of natural light, and which gives me free and frequent access to being outdoors and spending time with nature. Now, when I go to "work" environments and see the fluorescent lights and the sterile, unnatural surroundings, I'm truly overwhelmed with gratitude that I have chosen not to spend the bulk of my life in such physical environments. This is a choice available to virtually everyone.

I encourage you to consider yourself in a unique situation. Like snowflakes, no two persons or families are exactly alike; and thus, your decisions to un-job yourself will need to be tailored to your specific situation, interests, and proclivities. Because of this, I have refrained from giving great amounts of details about my personal choices, and I've given you only a small, but varied sampling of how other people are un-jobbing.

Look at your *true needs*. Look at your *reserves and resources*. Look at your *talents and gifts*. Be clear about *what kinds of activities are truly joyful* for you, and what kinds of activities are not. Look into as many aspects as possible of whatever course of action you are considering. Develop a loving community of support. Be a part of others' loving community of support. (I believe that humans are in their basic nature tribal animals. Helping others in their un-jobbing process would be of great benefit to your own path.) Then you can put things all together in a constantly evolving, values-aligning progression. Remember, you will never feel like you have "arrived." *Everything* is in the journey.

In fact, a great idea is to join or start a Voluntary Simplicity Group, something which is already being done in some parts of the US and I'm sure in other Western countries as well. This is not a formal "organization" per se with projects and the like. The purpose is to get a group of people together who can support one another, offer ideas for solutions to problems which group members bring up, and to study books and other materials which can give people ideas and—no less important—inspiration. All of this is a way to encourage each member of the group to travel further down the path of personal alignment. A Voluntary Simplicity Group could begin with as few as 2 or 3 people. Meet regularly, and you will find that the whole is always greater than the sum of the parts!

Whatever exploring you do, though, do it with great patience. Give yourself plenty of time and by all means, make your moves only at the pace which feels good to you. Choose with freedom and total awareness. Never choose out of a sense of entrapment. Only do that which feels joyous and makes sense to *you*. Remember, this is *joyful* simplicity, not sacrificial simplicity. Absolutely refuse any feeling of deprivation!

Acting freely according to our fullest possible awareness is our inalienable right. That is what enables us to take charge of our own affairs, to become co-creators with the Higher Power of the Universe and raise ourselves and the rest of humanity toward our true, natural state—great and lasting joy and peace in harmony with our planet.

Happy un-jobbing!

AFTERWORD

Dear readers,

I have deliberately written a short book. My idea was to make the message here as succinct, direct, and easily accessible as possible. However, there are many things to think over when you contemplate the life-changing ideas that are discussed here. So, I invite you to consider the following:

If you want more details about the thoughts and ideas expressed in this book, consult the Appendix that follows. In it, I list a handful of organizations and publications which I consider to be very helpful for "un-jobbers." These organizations and publications are also doing meaningful work for this planet and its inhabitants. As such, they are worthy of your knowing about them and your supporting them. In addition, I include a bibliography of books which will beautifully supplement this book. This is a list of books many of which "blew me away" and changed my life. How grateful I am to the creators of these books. Read them, and enjoy the mind blowing. These books represent great ideas and material for study in a Voluntary Simplicity Support Group.

Hopefully, within the Appendix and the resources to which the Appendix will lead you, you will find the further help you need. If your problem is how to be more frugal, then you should find good resources here. If you're interested in the tax issue, or more ecological living, or philosophy, or inspiration, or how to earn income outside of major employment—all of these subjects can be found in the resources listed in the Appendix. Many of the publications will contain stories of other people "un-jobbing." And, since everyone's story is unique, someone else's story may be just what you need to move ahead.

Finally, I invite you to share your ideas, concerns, questions, miracles, or whatever with me as you go through your own un-jobbing. We all learn from communicating with one another. In fact, one good way to articulate how you *really* feel about something, is to put your thoughts and feelings down in writing. I am also interested in speaking and doing workshops based on this book. You can contact me c/o Free Choice Press at: PO Box 1027, Lexington, KY 40588-1027. I am also accessible by email at <mfogler@igc.apc.org>.

Peace to you,

M.F. Lexington, Kentucky,
Fall, 1996

APPENDIX

This Appendix is an annotated listing of organizations and books which I believe are particularly relevant to someone thinking about "un-jobbing." Obviously, there are many, many more organizations and books which also could be on this list. And, the organizations and books listed here will undoubtedly lead you to others, some that I may not know about. New books are coming out on this topic all the time. You are not alone in your interest in this.

I strongly recommend this list, however; and, I believe that this list will be an excellent jumping off place (at the very least) for your own personal explorations. It is important to remember that within our collective wisdom—the organizations, books, and other people that we connect with, plus our own selves!—there is everything we need to know. The true answers are always within, or at least within our grasp. As the saying goes, "when the student is ready, the teacher appears."

ORGANIZATIONS/PUBLICATIONS

Aquarian Research Foundation, 1620 Morton Street, Philadelphia, PA 19144. This group is particularly concerned with creating a society of small, self-reliant, cooperative communities. They publish a gutsy, highly thought-provoking newsletter as well disseminate a Directory of Intentional Communities and many other materials.

Center for Nonviolence & Voluntary Service, PO Box 1058, San Jacinto, CA 92383. The CNVS educates on the Gandhian message of nonviolence and how urgently important it is to incorporate this message into our personal lives. What would you do with your life if you didn't have a major job? Connect with this organization. They have wonderful ideas for voluntary service and ways to live the Gandhian idea of the Law of Love. (See below for an excellent little book they disseminate.)

Co-op America, 1850 M Street NW, Suite 700, Washington, DC 20036. This organization works very hard to get what business we insist on having to be as "green" and "socially responsible" as possible. An important group in the Co-op movement, it publishes *Co-op America Quarterly* which is very worthwhile reading.

EarthSave Foundation, 706 Frederick Street, Santa Cruz, CA 95062. Specializing in educating about the connection of diet to your health, your values, and the environment, EarthSave really tells it like it is with gentleness, directness, and clarity. This is a very worthy group, giving a must understanding for a simple, meaningful lifestyle. The founder is John Robbins (an author cited below) who was heir to the Baskin-Robbins ice cream empire. He turned down the family business (and fortune) and spent years researching the connection of the human diet with the planet and the well-being of all living things on the planet. The result is the ongoing work of this fine organization and the two books cited below.

Friends of Peace Pilgrim, 43480 Cedar Avenue, Hemet, CA 92344. Connect with these folks for pure inspiration. They publish and give away (not sell, although donations are gratefully accepted) writings by a true modern avatar, a woman who called herself Peace Pilgrim. (See more details about her in the Bibliography below.) You can get books, booklets, audio tapes, and videos. There is also an occasional newsletter. All are wonderfully pure, simple, inspiring truth.

The Global Cooperative Society, Rainbow Lodge, RR 1 Box 1377, Buckingham, VA 23921. Can we change the present global competitive system to a total global cooperative society? This organization—which can be joined for a minimum of $1 US per year—has a plan. It involves all of us, as individuals, one by one by one by one…to spread the principles of cooperation within all the organizations we belong to: *democracy* in decision making and *justice* in the sharing of benefits.

The National War Tax Resistance Coordinating Commiittee, PO Box 774, Monroe, ME 04951-0774. Besides helping citizens across the country to redirect their taxes away from militarism and toward peace, this organization has a helpful literature piece on simple living as it relates to taxes.

The New Road Map Foundation, PO Box 15981, Seattle, WA 98115.   NRM encourages financial independence through frugality and simplicity, in order that one's life can truly serve oneself and the common good.   Their program to achieve financial independence, many of the points from which are featured in this book, is overall quite excellent.   Their advice to invest in US Treasury bonds is ethically questionable, but their taped course and the book *Your Money or Your Life* (see Bibliography below) are otherwise excellent and extremely useful and practical.

The Peace Taxpayers, PO Box 333, Nellysford, VA 22958. Does the name "peace taxpayers" sound like a contradiction in terms?   Not according to this organization.   They have very helpful information and inspiration to help you get your tax paying in alignment with your values—and without waiting for the proverbial act of Congress to take place first.   There is no need to wait for mass consciousness to catch up with your own consciousness!

Positive Futures Network, PO Box 10818 Bainbridge Island, WA 98110. This organization educates and researches on sustainable lifestyles. Their journal, *Yes! A Journal of Positive Futures* is superb, and often brings issues down to the personal level that's very meaningful and useful. It's great, cutting-edge reading.

E.F. Schumacher Society, 140 Jug End Road, Great Barrington,

MA 01230. This organization educates on the "small is beautiful" economic ideas of E.F. Schumacher (see book listed below). They have publications and conferences on such topics as decentralized economic organization, local currencies, and community land trusts.

Simple Living Quarterly, 2319 N. 45th Street, Box 149, Seattle, WA 98103. A fine quarterly journal, with articles about people doing the kinds of things discussed in this book. It's worthwhile reading. We are not alone!

BIBLIOGRAPHY

As any good student of un-jobbing practices, always remember to check with public libraries and friends and acquaintances, if at all possible, before you buy a book. (Unless, of course, you really want your own copy to refer back to or to loan to your friends, etc.)

Benson, Bill, *The Law That Never Was*. Available from Constitutional Research Associates, PO Box 550, South Holland, IL 60473. You won't find this book in any publicly-funded library (for obvious reasons), but if you want to read the findings of two men who took the trouble to travel to all 48 states involved with the ratification process of the 16th Amendment (which supposedly "legalized" the federal income tax), you can get all the details of their research in this book. It's not bargain priced, but the book will put our federal income tax situation in a new light, and perhaps give you new meaning to the idea of government fraud.

Callenbach, Ernest, *Ecotopia*, Berkeley, CA: Banyan Tree Books, 1975. As you can see, this is now a dated book. And, while there is plenty in the book which seems to be there merely for its entertainment value, there are great political and personal ideas contained herein which are not obsolete by any means.

Carter, Forrest, *The Education of Little Tree*. Albuquerque, NM: University of New Mexico Press, 1986. This is a wonderful book, based on the childhood of the author who was raised by his grandparents in the rural South. There is much to ponder here, about what true living and true education are all about. This is a book to treasure.

Chopra, Deepak, *Ageless Body, Timeless Mind*. New York: Harmony Books, 1993. Are you still worried that you need health insurance to have a long, healthy life? Read this myth-shattering book. It could change your life—or certainly the way you look at it. The main premise is that our bodies are not like machines which typically break down with more use. On the contrary, our bodies, according to Chopra, get better with more use (up to a sensible point, of course). We don't have to think of ourselves as being on a sure and certain linear progression of physical decline!

Dacyczyn, Amy, *The Tightwad Gazette: Promoting Thrift as a Viable Alternative Lifestyle*. New York: Villard Books, 1992. A zillion and one ideas from A to Z and from the ridiculous to the sublime on how to reduce the amount of money you spend. The main thrust here is not about simplicity, but merely about reducing expenses. There's something in here that is useful for everybody. (F.Y.I., the author's last name is pronounced like the word "Decision.")

de Mallac, Guy, *Gandhi's Seven Steps to Global Change.* Santa Fe, NM: Ocean Tree Books, 1989. Like the Peace Pilgrim organization, de Mallac's Center for Nonviolence and Voluntary Service (see above for address and other information) gives away this book (while accepting donations). It succinctly describes the timeless truth and wisdom of Gandhian nonviolence, and provides dozens of thoughtful ideas on ways to be of service to the planet and the life on it.

Dominguez, Joseph R, and **Robin, Vicki**, *Your Money or Your Life.* New York: Viking, 1992. Based on the very fine taped course from The New Road Map Foundation (see above), this book gives you some real tools to un-job, with plenty of details. (See other pertinent comments under the entry for the Foundation above.)

Elgin, Duane, *Voluntary Simplicity: An Ecological Lifestyle That Promotes Personal and Social Renewal.* New York: Bantam Books, 1988 (Originally published in hardcover by William Morrow). Long-winded and somewhat academic, it nonetheless does a great job giving the context and background for understanding the simple lifestyle. It clearly explains the difference between creating common good through large bureaucracies and creating common good through local self-reliance. As well, it explains the difference between "unfortunate, deprived poverty" and voluntarily- and consciously-chosen joyful simplicity.

Everett, Melissa, *Making a Living While Making a Difference,* New York: Bantam Books, 1995. This is a good book on the subject of "right livelihood," although it is somewhat conventional in its use of "career" terminology.

Friends of Peace Pilgrim, *Peace Pilgrim: Her Life and Work in Her Own Words.* Santa Fe, NM: Ocean Tree Books, 1982, 1988. The woman who called herself Peace Pilgrim was one of the most eloquent examples of someone who totally let go of fear and "walked her talk." In fact, she literally walked tens of thousands of miles—with no possessions or money—speaking the message of peace and simplicity. Well worth the inspiration. (See above under organizations—Friends of Peace Pilgrim—for ordering information.)

Gatto, John Taylor, *Dumbing Us Down: The Hidden Curriculum of Compulsory Schooling.* Philadelphia: New Society Publishers, 1992. This book is incredible and powerful in its impact. School is our society's preparation for the jobbing, Gross Domestic Product lifestyle. It's the equivalent of the job for children. We need to un-school as well as un-job, and this book effectively and powerfully tells you why. You may experience something like a "present life regression" reading this book. It's mind-blowing and life-changing. You'll realize why our society is where it is right now. A must read.

Ingram, Catherine, *In the Footsteps of Gandhi: Conversations with Spiritual Social Activists.* Berkeley, CA: Parallax Press, 1990. This book consists of introductions about, and interviews with, 12 remarkable "walk their talk" people—like

The Dalai Lama, Diane Nash, Mubarak Awad, Ram Dass, Cesar Chavez, etc. A wonderful, insightful, fantastic book. The book has deep insights into conscious living. It's a book that I've dipped back into repeatedly.

Kelley, Linda, *Two Incomes and Still Broke?* New York, NY: Times Books, a division of Random House, Inc., 1996. This is an extremely useful book about the financial costs of employment. It seems to leave no stone unturned, and clearly shows that more (gross) income or more people in a household being wage earners does not mean having more spendable money. There is also a good discussion on the tax code as it relates to income earning.

Kohn, Alfie, *No Contest: The Case Against Competition; Why We Lose in Our Race to Win*. Boston: Houghton Mifflin, 1986. An impressive, well-written, well-researched book which totally shatters the myths about humans being innately violent and competitive, and the alleged benefits of competition. This will change the way you look at humanity and at life, economically and otherwise.

Long, Charles, *How to Survive Without a Salary: Living the Conserver Lifestyle*. Warwick Publishers, 1992. Here you'll find lots of great ideas on how to live well with little money coming in or out. There are many ideads about how to earn your "casual income." No one will like all the suggestions, but the book is excellent to get your thoughts churning, and it accomplishes this with a delightful, humorous style.

Millman, Dan, *Way of the Peaceful Warrior*. Tiburon, CA: HJ Kramer, Inc. This is a fictionalized account of one person's spiritual journey. It's quite moving as well as highly entertaining. There are great messages about how to navigate through life with joy and simplicity. As it says on the cover, it's a book that changes lives. You'll smile all the way to your joyous core.

Morgan, Marlo, *Mutant Message Downunder*. New York: HarperCollins Publishers, 1994. This book takes you on a journey of an American physician wandering with an Aborigine tribe across the island continent of Australia. It's published as a novel; and there is some controversy as to whether or not the story is based on an actual experience of the author's. That controversy is a bit disappointing, and the accuracy about aboriginal life is questionable. Nonetheless, it's a powerful book with a deep message to ponder. Your mind will be swimming with new thoughts.

Nearing, Helen and Scott, *Living the Good Life*. New York: Schocken Books, 1970, Galahad Books, 1974. You may not want to go "back to the land," but the simplicity, truth, and sheer honesty of this book (and the two that follow) are absolutely wonderful and applicable to anyone's life. It describes how the Nearings lived their long and happy lives with great consciousness. If you are into things like gardening and house building, you will especially enjoy this and the following books. Regardless, these books are highly recommended.

Nearing, Helen and Scott, *Continuing the Good Life*. New York: Schocken Books, 1979. See comments for *Living the*

Good Life above.

Nearing, Helen, *Loving and Leaving the Good Life*. Post Mills, VT: Chelsea Green Publishers, 1992. This was written by Helen after Scott's leaving the good life. If you've read the other Good Life books, this one will be especially poignant and beautiful. Conscious living goes all the way through "death."

Quinn, Daniel, *Ishmael*. New York: Bantam Books, 1990. Winner of a Ted Turner Award (which attracted more than 2300 entries) for fiction with a strong ecological message for our time. A man finds his "teacher" who clearly delineates two kinds of people—Takers and Leavers. Obviously, western, "growth economics" cultures are Takers. A great read. The author really sheds light on the imprisoning aspect of the western Taker lifestyle. He argues that much of what we do, in efforts to improve our lives, is merely improving "prison conditions." Instead, we should be making efforts to leave the prison altogether! (i.e. un-jobbing!) Lots to ponder.

Robbins, John, *Diet for a New America*. Walpole, NH: Stillpoint Publishing, 1987. Since everyone eats frequently, this category of consumption and purchasing has major ramifications for our individual and collective lives. In that regard, I consider this book to be one of the most important works of this century. It's well-written, impeccably-documented, and all without sermonizing. Claim your own health and help planet Earth at the same time. Must reading.

Robbins, John, *May All Be Fed: Diet for a New World*. New

York: William R. Morrow, Inc., 1992. This book builds upon *Diet for a New America*, but with an added bonus: it helps you stock your kitchen and gives you fabulous recipes free of all animal products. A wise, clear, and delicious book.

Schumacher, E.F., *Small is Beautiful: Economics as if People Mattered*. New York: Perennial Library/Harper & Row, 1975. A long, but important book emphasizing how much we've strayed from structuring our lives on a small, human scale. (And, it's already more than 20 years old!) It shows how overgrown bureaucratic institutionalization affects our everyday personal lives, and documents alternatives to the large-scale ways which are still prevalent today, more than two decades later. Obviously, this book was ahead of its time. Since its publication, things have only gotten less small and beautiful. (See also listing above for the E.F. Schumacher Society.)

Sinetar, Marsha, *Do What You Love, the Money Will Follow: Discovering Your Right Livelihood*. New York: Paulist Press, 1987 and New York: Dell Publishing, 1989. The title alone makes this book worth having. It gives you good encouragement to "leap off the cliff" and follow your bliss.

Winter, Barbara, *Making a Living Without a Job: Winning Ways for Creating Work That You Love*. New York: Bantam Books, 1993. Like Melissa Everett's and Marsha Sinetar's books, this is another good book on the subject of "right livelihood," although it, too, is somewhat conventional in its use of "career" terminology.

Order extra copies of

Un-Jobbing

for your friends or your local library

Quantity discounts available:

1-9 copies	$9.95 each
10-24 copies	$8.50 each
25+ copies	$7.00 each

Shipping and Handling: $2 first book, $1 each book thereafter.

Quantity	Unit Price	Amount
KY residents add 6% sales tax		
Shipping and Handling		
TOTAL		

Make check payable to: FREE CHOICE PRESS
P.O. Box 1027
Lexington KY 40588-1027

(For shipping to countries outside the U.S., please inquire.)